Light One Candle

A Handbook for Bootstrapping Entrepreneurs

Michael Richards

First Edition

Innovation Press, Iowa City, Iowa USA

Light One Candle
A Handbook for Bootstrapping Entrepreneurs
By Michael Richards
Published by:
Innovation Press®
P.O. Box 975
Iowa City, Iowa 52244 USA

Copyright © 1998 by Michael Richards
Innovation Press® is a registered trademark

All rights reserved. No part of this book may be reproduced or transmitted in any form or by any means, electronic or mechanical, including photocopying, recording, or by any information storage and retrieval system, without the written permission of the Publisher, except for brief quotations in critical articles or press reviews.

This book is manufactured in the U.S.A.

Publisher's Cataloging-in-Publication
(Provided by Quality Books, Inc.)

Richards, Michael L.
    Light one candle: a guidebook for the bootstrapping entrepreneur/ by Michael Richards.--1st ed.
    p. cm.
    Preassigned LCCN: 97-77853
    ISBN: 1-891594-00-1

1. Entrepreneurship. 2. Small business--Management. 3. New business enterprises. I. Title.

HB615.R53 1998   658.4'21
                            QB197-41583

Dedicated to my entire family, and all the Candleworkers. Without the courage and perseverance of this entire team, my work would not have value or purpose. This book has one writer. We are *all* the author of this story.

Special thanks to the John Pappajohn Entrepreneurial Center and the Small Business Development Center at the University of Iowa, and the Ewing Marion Kauffman Foundation for the guidance provided for our entrepreneurial journey.

The only way we know how to express our gratitude to our most important mentor, Herb Wilson, is to pass on what he has given to Candleworks. That's the purpose of this book, to pass along our experience and support to other start-up entrepreneurs.

Bootstrapper's Basic Skills

Basic Skill #1: You are your most valuable asset. Place priority on investing in your own self worth.

Basic Skill #2: Start now! Doubt and procrastination are the major enemies of the bootstrap entrepreneur.

Basic Skill #3 By-pass all barriers. If a door shuts, climb through the window. If a flood rises, build a raft.

Basic Skill #4: Accept deferred gratification. In the early development of making your dream a reality, accept the *joy* of your work as your main pay.

Basic Skill #5: Make a *total* commitment. Without the passion of total enthusiastic commitment, you won't have the energy to transform your dream into reality.

Basic Skill #6: Discover the resources all around you. There are physical materials, creative ideas, time and knowledge being wasted all around you. Recycle!

Basic Skill #7: Base all of your work on love; love of yourself and family, love of your work, love of your co-workers and love of the customers you serve.

Basic Skill #8: Teamwork is the basis of all success. Success never happens alone. Build your team well.

Basic Skill #9: Make adversity your ally. Within every problem lie unclaimed jewels of opportunity.

Basic Skill #10: Build your work on a strong spiritual foundation. Faith will get you through it all.

Basic Skill #11: Live a healthy and balanced life.

Basic Skill #12: Network! Building alliances with other bootstrapping entrepreneurs increases your prospects for success. Communicate and connect.

Table of Contents

Chapter	Page
1. Bootstrapping Defined	1
2. The First Experiment	6
3. Creative Capitalization	17
4. Getting in on the Ground Floor	36
5. The Entrepreneurial Soup	50
6. Dumpster Diving	56
7. Profits through Principles	63
8. Each Worker has a Story	76
9. Turning Adversity into Advantage	104
10. Spiritual Entrepreneurship	117
11. Finding your Balance	127
12. Training, Support, Going Global	132

Open these pages and discover:

*how to transform your dream into an action plan

*how to overcome the barriers of fear and doubt

*how business can be the catalyst for social benefit

*how to market your plan in the global marketplace

In the midst of difficulty lies great opportunity.
  -ALBERT EINSTEIN

Notice and Disclaimer

This book was written to present an accurate, honest portrayal of the day to day life of an entrepreneur. This is our specific story, *the story of Candleworks.*

This book is not intended to define a particular course of action for you to follow if you launch your own enterprise. If any reader starts up their own business, we recommend that you first consult your own team of professional advisors for accounting, financing, legal, technical, and business management advice. *Risk is inherent in all private entrepreneurial endeavors.* If you decide to pursue a venture, such risk is the sole responsibility of the entrepreneur and any investors.

The purpose of this book is to educate and entertain. The author and Innovation Press shall have neither liability nor responsibility to any person or entity with respect to any loss or damage alleged to be caused, directly or indirectly by the information contained in this book. *Any risk is your responsibility.* If you do not wish to be bound by this **notice and disclaimer, you** may return this book to the publisher for a full refund.

Chapter One
Bootstrapping Defined

The man who moves a mountain begins by carrying small stones.
                    -ANCIENT CHINESE PROVERB

Onomatopoeia refers to words that mean what they *sound* like: Bang! Bootstrapping is a *visual word.* The meaning of Bootstrapping lies with the *image* it conjures up; *it looks like:* grabbing a hold just above your ankles to lift yourself up to something higher, something better. Bootstrappers build value from the ground up. They pull themselves up by their own bootstraps. Bootstrappers don't wait until they have enough money, enough time, enough talent or enough knowledge. They start exactly where they're at, with anything they've got. They simply get busy.

A bootstrapper thinks big, but starts very small. ***Light one candle.*** Take the first step, begin your journey. If you carefully plant your first seeds, the growth of your endeavor will grow naturally with care and love.

The first copies of this book were printed at the *unofficial* bootstrapper's headquarters, Kinko's copies! Kinko's is a great place to network with other start-up entrepreneurs. Why kowtow to a big publisher? Bootstrap your project into existence.

Bootstrapping means starting with exactly what you have to build your dream, even if what you have *appears to be nothing.* Real entrepreneurs create something out of nothing. Business bootstrappers are capitalists sans capital. They replace conventional capital with courage and creativity to launch novel enterprises. We usually think of a bootstrapper as someone who starts a business from scratch, the hard way. There are bootstrappers, however, in every human endeavor; the arts, science, and social organization. An athlete without obvious natural talent, who becomes a champion through desire, sheer force of will and diligent training is a bootstrapper. *A bootstrapper is anyone who has a dream and the courage to pursue it.* They don't let fear of unknown territory keep them from forging ahead.

> *Fear is a reaction.*
> *Courage is a decision.*
> -RAFE (IN "NEVER FEAR, NEVER QUIT")

A bootstrapper may not have a penny to start with. They discover, however, that they have *inner wealth* to draw on to produce something new and valuable in the world. This inner wealth includes deep reserves of passion, vision, creativity, dogged determination and raw power of will. This unlimited inner wealth produces visible outer wealth and success.

Bootstrappers may appear to the outside world, the doubters, cynics and naysayers around them, to have absolutely nothing. The secret of bootstrapping your way to success is realizing the *inner wealth* that you do have, and then using that personal wealth to create something totally new and exciting. No matter what your lot is in life, *build something on it*! The entire global chain of Marriott Hotels was started by a bootstrapping 26 year old with 9 seats in a little shack he operated as a rootbeer stand! There are *no excuses*.

Having no external resources at first can actually be a great windfall to the bootstrapping entrepreneur. With no outer, obvious resources with which to build a business, realize a vision, or launch an artistic career, the bootstrapper discovers their inner wealth out of *absolute necessity.* Often, the only way a bootstrapper survives is by sheer creativity and resourcefulness!

After a bootstrapper gains financial resources, they will still have these creative resources. It's much harder for a business that starts with adequate financial resources to gain creative resources, than vice versa. Creative problem solving is a valuable skill.

A bank roll from investors has a limit. Inner resources have no limit. Inner wealth pours forth infinitely; if you develop the discipline to go deeper and deeper into your interior source. A creative enterprise built by bootstrapping has unlimited potential by it's very nature. If exterior success originates from this interior well, the possibilities are boundless. Once this deep well is tapped, it will flow on, unless the bootstrapper denies and shuts off this source through fear, false pride, greed, or dishonesty.

Remembering the roots of your bootstrap beginnings will keep your growing enterprise vital. Once you are successful, assisting other start-up bootstrappers will keep you in touch with the experience, realizations and understanding that you have developed through traveling the bootstrap path.

That's the purpose of this book; to pass our experience along: to inform and inspire other bootstrappers in every field of human accomplishment.

The secret of life is to have a task,
something you devote your entire life to...
and the most important thing is--
it must be something you cannot possibly do!
  -HENRY MOORE

Whatever your dream is, whoever you are, with whatever you have, start *today*. Procrastination has destroyed all of the great works of art, amazing music, new inventions and miracle cures that the world *should have known*. You have a rare gift. Find it and give it to the world now. **Light your candle.**

What we need are more people
who specialize in the impossible.
  -THEODORE ROTHKE

Dream. Work hard. Achieve "the impossible". Create something wonderful from what appears to the world as nothing, as you realize your *inner resources*. The impressive thing about Christopher Columbus wasn't that he discovered a New World, rather that he sailed off into the horizon on the faith that it was there.

The greatest gift of all is opportunity. Opportunity exists in equal measure for everyone that seeks it out. Knowledge creates opportunity. Seek knowledge wherever you can: books, school, travel, the internet, music, art, and conversations with experienced people. Don't hesitate to just take action. Trial and error is still an excellent teacher. The key to success is not making the same mistake more than two or three times! Learn from your mistakes, and you'll keep moving toward your goal. One absolute way to know how to do a thing right is to have tried all of the wrong ways first. Be fearless and get movin'!

> *People can be divided into three groups:*
> *-those who make things happen*
> *-those who watch things happen*
> *-and, those who wonder what happened!*
> -JOHN W. NEWBERN

Get off the side lines today. Run onto life's game field and *make something happen*! You have nothing to loose but your fear. Through action you'll tap into the deepest roots of the American psyche; the prototype American hero is the underdog, who without the advantages and resources of their opponents, bootstrap their way past all barriers to victory.

The United States itself emerged through classic bootstrapping moxie. This tiny underdog conclave of colonists had the raw courage and audacity to declare a revolution against the most powerful global empire of the time, Great Britain. The result is the most successful social and economic experiment the world has yet seen. Bootstrappers thrive in America, because America had its genesis as an entrepreneurial vision. Every new bootstrapper plants the seeds to renew this vision. Every dreamer that moves their plan into action keeps the vision vital and growing.

A plan is just a dream with a deadline!

What America sorely needs at this stage of our history is a dynamic political bootstrapper to organize a viable third party, *of, by and for the people*; to challenge the two headed Republicrat monster that is no longer accountable to the citizens. Thomas Jefferson advised that we need a revolution in each generation. We've skipped a few too many generations.

Bootstrapper's Basic Skill #1: You are your most valuable asset. Always place your highest priority on investing in your own self-worth. Nothing else pays a higher return.

Reader's notes:

What does bootstrapping mean to you?

What is your passion in life? How can you convert your source of passion into a source of profit?

What dreams are you ready to convert to action plans?

Chapter Two
The First Experiment: New York Stories

Problems are opportunities in disguise. If life gives you a lemon, make some delicious lemonade. An entrepreneur is by nature an optimist. A bootstrapper is a visionary that is also an activist. All the darkness in the world cannot extinguish the *light of one candle.*

Candleworks had its genesis as an experiment on the cold streets of New York City in the winter of 1993. Statistics from the U.S. Department of Housing and Urban Development show that an average American family is just two paychecks away from homelessness. Our family faced such vulnerability first hand.

The restaurant that I was managing in New York City had a suspicious late night electrical fire. The next day, the restaurant owners closed the business without any notice to their thirty employees. Overnight, I found myself jobless and without income in the city with the highest cost of living in America. Our family had no savings. We were literally just those two proverbial paychecks away from homelessness.

We were living in a dilapidated, five story, walk-up tenement on New York's notorious Lower East Side. New York's real estate inflation bubble of the early 1990's had just burst. All maintenance on our building ceased. The household garbage of the building was left to stack up outside the entrance door. Crack dealers haunted the lobby. Without notice, our landlord abandoned our building. All utilities were shut off, and the seven families in tenancy found ourselves literally in the dark one night. The heat was off, the building got very cold. There was no running water for showers, washing dishes, or cooking.

Three of seven tenants bailed out of the abandoned, decaying building within a few days. Rather than face actual street-level homelessness, the Richards family organized the remaining four tenants into an ad-hoc tenant's association. We set up a rotating work schedule to maintain hallways, shovel snow and dispose of the building's refuse. We placed all building utility accounts in our own name. We all assumed squatter's rights on the run-down structure. Rain was literally coming in through the roof. All the tenants pooled our limited resources for tar and rolls of roofing. We sealed up the building with a Saturday work party. Instead of giving in to homelessness, our family became self-sufficient urban homesteaders.

Our family realized that if *we* were personally that vulnerable to homelessness, something had to be done for low-income families to create economic self-sufficiency. Neither handouts to homeless persons on the street, nor traditional government welfare programs could ever solve the growing problem of poverty and homelessness in America. We needed a modern day application of the ancient Chinese proverb: *"Give a man a fish, he'll eat for a day. Teach him to fish, he'll eat for a lifetime."* Thus, the Candleworks idea was born.

EARLY ALLIANCES

I had lost my job without notice. Fortunately, our family of six still had my wife's income. This provided greatly needed, yet inadequate support in this expensive city. Lynette worked as the retail store manager for one of the very first locations opened by an innovative British company, The Body Shop. They had just expanded their business to the United States. The Body Shop had gained international attention as a creative company that integrated social responsibility with bottom line financial performance. Outside the very doorstep of The Body Shop's upscale Upper Eastside Manhattan shop that Lynette managed, homeless people had set up a curbside camp. I was organizing educational opportunities for homeless persons living in a shelter in East Harlem. Lynette and I combined our experience and contacts to create the first Candleworks experiment.

Lynette and I didn't have a single quarter to spare for the daily solicitations from the homeless persons that we literally had to step over to get down the street to her place of employment. We did however, take the time to stop and talk; to accept street people with the value of person to person recognition and conversation. We set up a meeting with Body Shop Corporate managers and presented a novel idea: how about applying The Body Shop's commitment to social responsibility at a very basic street level?

After several negotiations, we had a commitment from The Body Shop management to test candles as an appropriate consumer product that would be complementary to their company's line of natural personal care products. The Body Shop agreed to test market our first candle product in just the single store that Lynette managed.

Our goal was to create jobs for homeless families. We had no capital to create a conventional product manufacturing business. The product we created to meet this need were simple hand-rolled beeswax candles. Hand-rolled candles could be made without any expensive manufacturing equipment. Our only tools were the hands of homeless families. We made candles in lively colors that were complementary to the presentation of other Body Shop products. Our candles were packed into The Body Shop's colorful gift baskets of soaps, shampoos and lotions.

We literally took the last few hundred dollars our family had to buy several boxes of beeswax. We launched this experimental enterprise in the cramped kitchen of our own tenement apartment. We walked into a neighborhood soup kitchen that served homeless people on the street and simply asked:

"Who wants to work today?" Homeless people came home with us and went to work. In our kitchen, these work sessions took on the convivial nature of an old fashioned quilting bee; everyone doing their part, while jiving, joking and laughing. Body Shop customers responded enthusiastically to both our products and the community project that created them.

The Richards family is a group of "never quit" survivors. Our attitude is that poverty is a state of mind, not a low bank balance. We've tapped our wealth of motivation and creativity to create opportunity for ourselves and other people who are facing challenging financial and personal circumstances. We model commitment and perseverance in our work.

A very fortuitous situation developed. The Body Shop that Lynette managed was designated as a training location for new franchise owners that had purchased rights to operate Body Shop stores in locations all over the United States. The new franchise owners observed how well the customers responded to the colorful Candleworks products in this one store. By popular demand, the Body Shop Corporate managers agreed to designate Candleworks candles as an approved accessory product. This decision was made in November right at the peak of the busy Holiday retail season. Scores of Body Shop franchise operators all over the country rushed in orders. In a matter of weeks, our tiny New York tenement apartment became a makeshift manufacturing facility, warehouse and U.P.S. shipping terminal. Stacks of beeswax, wick, packaging materials and finished candles first filled our own apartment to the ceiling, and then were stacked out into the shared hallways of our building. This desolate building in a depressed urban neighborhood became a cheerful, bustling beehive.

Two blocks away from our own abandoned building, several activist nuns had set up a very dynamic urban homesteading team, Nazareth Homes. Nazareth Homes organized "sweat equity" labor to reclaim abandoned tenement buildings in our neighborhood for cooperative permanent housing for homeless families. Lynette and I walked into their crowded community headquarters to propose a working alliance. Over the desk of Sister Marian was a tattered sign that read: "PRAY FOR THE DEAD. WORK LIKE HELL FOR THE LIVING!" *With that attitude, we knew we were in the right place.*

Our tiny family apartment and hallways were already overflowing with materials. Busy homeless families made candles in our cramped kitchen. Sister Marian offered the basement of one of their urban homesteads as a temporary workshop and warehouse for Candleworks. As a fair trade, we created employment opportunities for formerly homeless families now in residence at Nazareth Homes. In just one month before Christmas, Candleworks churned out tens of thousands of candles for Body Shop stores in a hundred cities around the U.S. All of the formerly homeless families had their best Christmas in years. Rent, phone and utility bills were paid on time. Happy children had gifts under their Christmas trees.

Candleworks sponsored a Christmas Party for all of the families living at Nazareth Homes. We invited The Body Shop to donate festive holiday gift baskets of shampoos, soaps and lotions for each family. If you've never been homeless, it's easy to take for granted the refreshing pleasure of a warm shower. These body care gifts were as precious to these families as the gifts of gold, frankincense and myrrh on the very first Christmas. We all had a joyous send-off celebration for one of the homeless teenage candlemakers. She had saved her holiday candle earnings to pay for a trip to participate in a national cello competition. She played a concerto as we all wandered off into the snowy New York night. The Christmas before, she and her mother were both homeless on the streets of Manhattan.

Nazareth Homes had reclaimed and renovated about a dozen deteriorating buildings and former crack dens in our neighborhood. One building was set aside for homeless mothers who also had serious drug and alcohol problems. Child protective authorities had taken custody of their children. The purpose of this cooperative home was to rebuild their lives, get drug free and re-unite the mothers with their children. One resident had been a street alcoholic and drug addict for several years. This year, she used her candlemaking earnings to purchase fine fabric along Manhattan's Seventh Avenue Fashion District. She launched her own cottage industry making silk scarves for exclusive New York boutiques. Her self-esteem and hope grew. *She was back in life's game.*

All winter long, we continued to wheel tons of beeswax around the neighborhood with our only company vehicle: a two-wheel handcart I bought from a used furniture dealer in the neighborhood. Several years later, this very first "company vehicle" still wheels tons of wax around our present candle factory. In a given day, I'd lug over a ton of wax by hand, up five stories of steep, dark stairways of crumbling tenements on the mean streets of New York's notorious Alphabet City. Corner drug dealers would greet me along the way as I made my rounds. In these old run-down buildings, homeless mothers and children set up in temporary shelters made candles to earn their own money to buy groceries, baby formula and pay their utility bills. A few days later, I'd re-trace the same route in the neighborhood rolling my hand cart. I'd make several trips up and down the creaky stairs to haul tons of finished candles back downstairs. I'd then cart the load over to the temporary shipping room in the basement of Nazareth Homes. Candleworks is definitely a business built with "sweat equity"!

In that first season of work, we'd wheel our two hand-cart through Tompkins Square Park, where several hundred homeless people had been set up for several years in an urban shanty town constructed of cardboard, tin, and throw-away lumber. Hundreds of riot-control cops in armored vehicles had recently stormed the park and drove the homeless people out of their urban camp into a vacant lot just two blocks away. Chain link and barb-wire barriers were then placed around the park. Tompkins Square was patrolled by hundreds of police for most of that year to keep the homeless squatters out.

Millions of dollars were spent to carry out this urban quasi-military operation. A local Irish priest in the neighborhood told me it looked just like the operations of the British military in Northern Ireland. We wondered what could have been accomplished if those same multiple millions of dollars would have been invested productively into community economic development? Homeless squatters in the park could have thus earned their own money to rent permanent shelter and become self-sufficient. One urban radical had stenciled on the park walkway: *"Build an Army of the Poor."* Candleworks converted the meaning of this radical political slogan to build a neighborhood army dedicated to *economic* rather than political revolution. The City of New York's official response to the homeless gathered in Tompkins Square was based on *fear and force.* Candleworks created a novel response based on *love and trust.*

The growing light of Candleworks provided a vital contrasting demonstration of how minimal resources could be used to build community based economic development. We demonstrated a way to solve deep rooted problems that costly welfare and police control could not solve. The New York Times came and documented our work in the Sunday Business Section. The New York Daily News interviewed teenage homeless mothers working with Candleworks about the failure of the welfare system and their success as candlemakers. Television crews came and interviewed Candle Project participants for the evening news.

Visitors from all over the U.S. came to see this working model of community economic development. A delegation came from England. They returned home to launch a work project for homeless people on the streets of London modeled on Candleworks.

Newt, Bill and the Capitol Hill gang were all competing to deliver welfare reform rhetoric to gain political advantage. Candleworks delivered the *real goods*. We demonstrated how bootstrap entrepreneurial economic development could actually create a viable alternative to welfare at the *street level*. We left the old welfare bureaucracy completely out of our loop. We built a new socio-economic paradigm based on self-sufficiency.

Sales that first year reached nearly $100,000! With very little start-up capital, we had proven that with just courage, hard work and ingenuity a private enterprise could be launched to create economic self-reliance for disadvantaged and disabled persons. This initial experimental stage of Candleworks had proven successful. *Now it was time to organize this viable idea into a working full-scale manufacturing business.*

In April, Nazareth Homes informed Candleworks that the basement they had loaned to us as a temporary warehouse was now needed to warehouse furniture donations. Nazareth Homes had been soliciting items to furnish all of the new apartments for homeless families that they had renovated. Candleworks began a search for a commercial space to set up a permanent manufacturing location. We quickly discovered that with the exorbitant price of commercial real estate in New York City, this was not financially feasible. *Candleworks was at a crucial crossroads.* We'd hit a major road block, so we looked for a detour. The sign pointed west, *to Iowa.*

The Better Homes Fund, a private charity set up to assist homeless families, was established by Better Homes and Gardens Magazine. David Jordan, the Editor in Chief of Better Homes and Gardens was one of the founders of this charity. He had heard about the innovative work of homeless families working in Candleworks from Garrett Douglas. Garrett had been a Wall Street investment banker. He left that world to live a simpler life on Cape Cod in Massachusetts. Garrett was the first person that contacted us after our work with homeless families was reported in the New York Times. At Garrett's invitation, Mr. Jordan traveled from The Better Homes and Garden's headquarters in Iowa to New York to observe our work first hand. We negotiated a creative alliance. Candleworks produced a special holiday gift pack of candles that the Better Homes Fund could market to raise funds for the charity. Through a full page display ad, these candles were offered to the readers of Better Homes and Gardens magazine as a *"gift that gives twice";* opportunities for employment were provided to homeless families making the candles, and profits were donated to the Better Homes Fund to assist homeless families all over the U.S.

Garrett Douglas was inspired by what he observed at Candleworks. He launched a similar work project for homeless families, *Cape Cod Works*, based on the Candleworks model. *Cape Cod Works* set up a novel enterprise to package scented glycerin soaps.

Meredith Corporation, publisher of Better Homes and Gardens is based in Des Moines, Iowa. Lynette and I were originally from Iowa. We made a Holiday visit to see our families in Iowa. We stopped in for a follow-up meeting with David Jordan at the Meredith Publishing home office in Des Moines. We set up a plan for a new fund raising product offering in the Mother's Day edition of Better Homes and Gardens magazine; a gift basket with rose scented candles and rose scented soaps from Cape Cod Works.

Our next important alliance was created when Garrett Douglas set up a three way meeting of entrepreneurial minds; Candleworks, Cape Cod Works and Jill Nadina. Jill is the founder of a very innovative and socially responsible company that makes an all purpose body creme from natural ingredients. **Nadina's Cremes** are for use on hands, face, etc., and come in numerous delightful scents. **Nadina's Cremes** are a unique product. They are packaged in exquisite little hand made ceramic jars made by local potters. Nadina's Cremes, Candleworks and Cape Cod Works launched a joint effort. We formed an alliance to distribute products from all three organizations. Nadina's Cremes had been developed from a tiny bootstrap venture. Jill started by peddling her cremes out of the back of a station wagon. Nadina's Cremes are now sold in more than 1,000 exclusive boutiques all over the U.S.

With these new alliances, Candleworks started to grow very rapidly. We'd realized that commercial space for the permanent development of Candleworks was much too expensive in New York City. We searched for permanent manufacturing facilities in Iowa. We leased a small building in Iowa City in 1994. In New York, the experimental stage of development of Candleworks had provided just part-time supplemental income for our participants. Our long-term goal was to expand Candleworks so that it could provide stable full-time employment opportunities for disadvantaged and disabled persons, and our own family.

Our donated work space was no longer available. We converted our New York employment organization to home-based cottage industry. Formerly homeless candlemakers worked in their apartments in Nazareth Home's buildings. Candleworks moved to permanent facilities in Iowa City. We kept this cottage industry active in New York City during a one year transitional phase. Candlemakers in New York continued to work part-time as they gradually found other permanent employment. Candleworks phased out the New York experiment and began to establish a full-scale candle manufacturing enterprise in Iowa City. *A new chapter was ready to begin.*

Bootstrapper's Basic Skill #2: Start now! Doubt and procrastination are the major enemies of the bootstrap entrepreneur. Conquer doubt and inaction with decisive, bold action.

> *Whatever you can do, or dream you can,*
> *begin it now.*
> *Boldness has genius, power and magic in it.*
> *-GOETHE*

Reader's notes:

What is the first action step you can take to launch your own bootstrap endeavor?

Who are your first allies for this venture?

What initial barriers do you need to overcome?

Chapter Three
Creative Capitalization: from Horse Trading to Movie Deals

To expand our experimental candle project into a full-scale candle manufacturing business, we needed seed capital. Local commercial banks were not interested at that point. Their basic response was: *"You're going to hire who? You're going to make what?"* Without start up capital, we set up our next candle production facility in an abandoned building. We gerry-rigged candle making equipment made with materials salvaged out of local construction dumpsters! In the conventional banking frame of reference, we had no collateral. Our workforce had traditionally been viewed as transient, troublesome, unreliable, and unemployable. That's a hard sell to a conservative Midwest banker! It's a hard sell to any banker.

When one door closes, another opens. While we were struggling with home and survival issues in New York City, our second oldest son, Ben had moved out to the West Coast to pursue his acting and writing career. He found a survival level job. Ben was also hanging one paycheck away from street level homelessness. He met lots of homeless kids on the streets of Santa Monica, California. Ben started to write about his experiences.

Ben used his meager paycheck to rent a dilapidated old garage. He converted it into a makeshift shelter for homeless kids. *"The Kids from Nowhere"* is Ben's real life story of this experience. As Ben celebrated his twenty-first birthday, Warner Brothers bought this inspirational screenplay. Rather than wait years for a full length feature film to be funded by this major Hollywood studio, Ben decided to take the bootstrap approach. He used the majority of his check from the screenplay to produce and direct a short version of his film with struggling young actors. He then invested the four thousand dollars that remained from his first Hollywood movie deal into expansion of Candleworks.

Candleworks creates candles as a private label manufacturer for progressive chains of retail stores. As a manufacturer of products, we had to acquire raw materials, pay our rent and other general overhead expenses and payroll. After we shipped to our customers, we'd bill them with standard industry "30 day net terms". We'd expect payment one month later (*in actuality*, it sometimes takes from 60 to 90 days to collect from our customers.) The total cycle to purchase raw materials, pay our workforce, deliver goods and collect requires a 90 to 120 day short term financing cycle. This was very challenging without financial backing from banks or investors.

In the beginning, all the development and growth of Candleworks was carried out with a classic bootstrap approach. We'd produce products as efficiently as possible, ship the candles and send out bills. Various members of our entrepreneurial family wore all of the management hats: Production Manager, Marketing Director, Accounting Manager. We all had executive jobs, *just no paychecks!* Just as soon as checks came in from our customers, most funds were immediately invested back into the business operation. We'd purchase more materials, pay overhead and payroll in a continuing cycle of growth and expansion.

Deferred gratification is a life skill unique to humans. During the start up years of our bootstrap venture, our family survived on a pittance. We ate simply, leased a small house and drove old cars. Entrepreneurship requires long range vision and short term austerity.

After the $4,000 investment provided by Ben's movie deal, we needed additional funds to purchase an expanding inventory of beeswax. Our customer base was growing exponentially. Lynette's father, Max, is an Iowa farmer. He sold a horse for $2,200, and loaned it to her so that we could purchase more beeswax. Candleworks kept expanding rapidly. Our oldest son, Michael invested $4,000 he saved while working as a waiter when he attended New York University. Our younger two sons Sol and Mel contributed by sweat equity. *We all did our part.*

During the next Christmas season, checks from customers were not arriving quickly enough to cover payroll. Lynette borrowed $10,000 against her Body Shop employee retirement plan and invested that into our business. My dad, Tom and my stepmother, Ruth each loaned 10 thousand dollars. Timely cash flow is the main challenge for a start-up business.

From year one to year three our sales grew 100% from approximately $100,000 to $200,000. From year two to three we experienced 300% growth to $600,000 in annual sales. Funding that kind of growth is very daunting. This year we're moderating our growth to a 100% rate. We expect to generate a million dollars in gross sales. In each year since inception, Candleworks has posted a book profit of at least 14%. *Book profit* is the operational word here. Surplus cash does not exist with this type of business growth. To the contrary, this growth creates a very challenging shortage of available working capital. Bootstrappers must discover creative ways to fund their growth.

Our business operates with an "open book" financial policy. All team members share in full disclosure financial reports. Since Candleworks is a private enterprise that operates in the public interest, people from the community, business leaders and local government officials are also welcome to participate in this "open book" process. Here's a little story I told one Friday afternoon to illustrate our cash flow challenge to all of our staff:

20

A BOOTSTRAPPER'S PARABLE

"Imagine a family facing imminent homelessness. To ward off family financial disaster, they pawn the few possessions they have and buy a cart full of beeswax. Along with a few homeless people from a local soup kitchen, the family make up a cart full of colorful candles. They start selling them on the street corner. The candles cost $70 to produce. They sell for $100. Everyone feels great! We've gotten back our original $70, plus a $30 profit! Shall we celebrate with pizza and a night at the movies for everyone? No, hold on; let's sacrifice immediate gratification and keep this thing going. Let's buy more wax and do it again."

Everyone nodded with interest. I continued the story:

"That's all fine and good, but now a crowd comes around the corner. They're so happy with the pleasant scent and joyful colors of our candles that they want to buy more, and now their friends and families want to buy candles too! The whole crowd want to buy $1000 worth of candles. All we have is 100 bucks (the original $70 and $30 profit). So how do we make $1,000 worth of candles to sell to all of these eager customers? That will take $700 to cover the cost of production. We'll get the $700 back and have a new profit of $300."

Our staff all smiled with recognition at this plight. We pop some popcorn and pass it around as I continue:

"Everyone goes with just one meal each day and pool their $100 savings. The whole group scans the entire neighborhood for returnable cans and bottles. That brings in another $80. We send the wax company our entire $180 and convince them that if they ship hundreds of dollars worth of wax we can profit together. We're confident that we can pay the balance due in one month, after we sell the candles. The wax company delivers. All the candlemakers get busy. A

month later we send hundreds of dollars to the wax company, then happily count our $300 profit. Wow!"

Everyone in the Candleworks team move up to the edge of their chairs to discover where this tale will lead.

I continue the story. *"Now a small mob comes around the next corner; old customers, new customers, friends and family now want to buy $10,000 worth of our hand-made candles. We've already learned how that works. With this kind of sales, we can look forward to $3,000 profit. We'll have to cross a giant hurdle first though; now we need $7,000 to cover the expenses to make this stock of candles for this eager market. We realize that this is the way of life of the bootstrapping entrepreneur. It takes money to make money.*

With another friendly call to the wax company, thousands of dollars worth of wax is placed on a truck, and heads down the road toward us as an act of faith and trust. It worked once, so the wax company thousands of miles away decides it's worth the risk to help build this growing wax customer into a bigger and bigger customer. It makes good business sense to work together."

"Wow, that sounds just like Candleworks!" Chuck said.

Setting up strategic alliances for mutual profit with your suppliers and customers is probably the single most important skill for successful bootstrapping. The fact of the matter is that most operational capital in the American economy is provided from one business to another through short term financing of goods and services. This accounts for much more business capital than all banks and the stock market combined. The entire structure of our economy depends on thousands of small businesses trusting other small businesses to keep the wheels of commerce turning. Small businesses create most new jobs and create the majority of growth activity in our economy. Small businesses *generate* economic value. Conglomerates, banks and governments usurp much of the value created by small entrepreneurs through taxation, interest, mergers and buyouts.

We got back to the family and their candle cart story:

*"The first family of bootstrappers are now followed by a growing parade of candlemakers and eager buyers. Everyone joins into this carnival of commerce. That first small mob becomes a big mob. Now they want to buy $100,000 worth of candles. So do your math; we can create thousands of dollars of profit to create economic self-reliance for scores of homeless and disabled people, if we can just find a way to finance **$70,000** of operating expenses. From the first $70 we needed for our start-up to $70,000 operating cash is a giant leap!"*

At the end of this story hour, our entire staff understood the challenges of business better than most newly graduated M.B.A. students. Life 101 isn't taught in Business Schools. Bootstrapping is learned by doing.

With the rapid growth of Candleworks, our need for capital expands exponentially. As I work on my lap-top computer to stack the sentences of this book into my word-processing system, our once tiny enterprise now needs hundreds of thousands of dollars of working capital each year. Our sales this year will be a million dollars! The same math works whether we're a start-up enterprise pushing our candle cart on the streets of New York or a full-scale manufacturing firm housed in a ten thousand square foot warehouse in Iowa.

In the spring of 1994, we received our single largest order to date; a $15,000 purchase order for Mother's Day gift baskets of candles from the Better Homes Fund. Candleworks had just recently moved into an abandoned building that we converted into a creative chandlery. Our staff wired-up the old shack for electrical power. The small work team of candlemakers let out a hoot of delight as this order came over the fax machine. *Better Homes and Gardens* magazine sold these gift baskets through a full-page display in their May issue to raise funds to assist other homeless families all over the country.

A local metal shop had just completed fabrication of our first piece of industrial equipment, steam jacket wax melting tanks. This project had required the use of *all* of our available operating capital. We didn't have funds to hook up running water, so we carried hundreds of gallons of water from a well down the road to operate our wax melter. Our bootstrapping venture looked more like a Third World Peace Corp project than a growing business in The United States of America.

The celebration of this large order merged into a sobering realization; how do we cover the $10,000 operating cash required to produce this order? The next day we were pondering a solution to this challenge. A fax then arrived from Body Shop Canada with their opening order for $20,000 worth of new custom made candles! Our $10,000 capitalization problem just became a $24,000 problem. A problem is just an opportunity in work clothes. We got to work.

Wendy Germain, Project Director for The Better Homes Fund contributed the East Coast moxie she had cultivated growing up on New York's Lower East Side. She realized that a large bank in our area was one of the major banks used by the charity's key corporate sponsor, Meredith Publications. She called the commercial lending officer of the local branch of this huge bank. She challenged the lending officer to invest back into their community. Since this request was coming from an organization linked with one of their important multi-million dollar corporate customers the banker decided to listen. When Wendy talks people tend to listen.

Candleworks pledged the proceeds of our two new purchase orders directly to the bank for repayment of a short-term $25,000 line of credit. We efficiently produced the orders for The Better Homes Fund and The Body Shop, Canada. By August we had paid off the entire loan *early*, in less than three months.

After a year of product development and negotiations with The Body Shop, Candleworks was selected to be the private label manufacturer of their new line of aromatherapy candle products for all 250 of their stores in the U.S. *This was a major coup.* Chemists in the research and development division of Body Shop International in Great Britain had been working on the formulation of a non-petrochemical wax blend that would be appropriate for aromatherapy candles. This team of professionals did not achieve the desired result. Most candles are made from petrochemical by-products and materials processed from animal fat. The Body Shop had taken a strong environmental stance counter to the petroleum industry and animal by-products. A non-petro natural wax was very important to the founder, Anita Roddick.

The development of this vegetable wax candle was originally let out for open bid to many of the largest candle manufacturers in the world. Body Shop executives in charge of purchasing were skeptical that a tiny, rag-tag, bootstrap operation like Candleworks could create the sophisticated wax blend that was required for their non-petro wax candles. Rolling pre-cut sheets of beeswax around a wick, arts and crafts style was within the comfort zone for Candleworks. For us to manufacture a sophisticated line of natural wax aromatherapy candles would require a major quantum leap in technical expertise.

After months and months of negotiation with The Body Shop, Candleworks was allowed to submit natural wax aromatherapy prototypes along with the major manufacturing firms. We went through dozens of rounds of sample submissions and evaluations. Finally, Candleworks received great news. Our natural wax formula and botanical oil scent formulas *were evaluated as the very best!* Better than had been developed by The Body Shop International's internal research and development team. Better than had been developed by many giant multi-million dollar candle manufacturing companies. Often, a small company is more motivated to create a superior product. This result was more important to us that to "the big guys". Our very existence depended on getting this work.

Everyone at Candleworks was elated. Body Shop, U.S.A. projected that they would order several hundred thousand aromatherapy candles each year. This would provide the opportunity we had been striving for; to create full-time, year 'round jobs, rather than just part-time supplemental income.

We were ready to go! Then we heard the unthinkable, that a <u>second choice</u> in the product based evaluations, *a very large commercial manufacturer* was selected to manufacture the new line of custom aromatherapy candles for all of The Body Shop U.S.A. stores. Body Shop management in the U.S. had decided that a small motley crew working in a tiny abandoned building just couldn't deliver the volume of product required.

I did not have the heart to take this discouraging news back to our room full of hopeful, hard-working candle crafters. They were all just a few months out of the homeless shelter, living happy and productive on their own for the first time in years. Success often only happens if we just *refuse to take no for an answer.* A real entrepreneur never gives up. After pondering this situation until the middle of the night, I tapped out a pre-dawn missive on my computer. I sent it zipping across the Atlantic instantaneously, via the FAX that sat on a wooden crate in our run-down shack, now recycled into a candle factory. I sent the

FAX directly to Anita Roddick, founder of The Body Shop. I appealed directly to her entrepreneurial spirit. She had started with humble bootstrap beginnings in one tiny little shop; and had grown into a multi-national giant that operates over a thousand stores in more than 40 countries! Within a few days, the word came back. Candleworks got the deal! Everyone leaped up and cheered.

The first order was for 60,000 candles. A three-hundred thousand dollar sale! Now, remember our lesson in Entrepreneurial Economics 101 about the family pushing the candle cart down the street? This sale could produce about a hundred thousand dollar profit to create more jobs for more people in need who were ready to work. First, however, we'd need about $200,000 in operating capital to deliver the goods. I worked out strategic alliances with raw material suppliers (one was our glass-supplier half-way around the world). These suppliers could make their share of profit from this significant sale if they delivered goods to Candleworks on direct trade credit. We'd then pay them after we were paid by The Body Shop. This direct business to business financing covered half of the $200,000 working capital required.

I mapped out detailed cash flow charts and a business plan on this new aromatherapy project. I went back to the major bank where we had just paid off our $25,000 loan. I clearly demonstrated that we required a $100,000 loan to carry out this new Body Shop contract efficiently. The bank officer got back to us: they would set up a line of credit for only $50,000.

In the banker's office, I wondered aloud at his logic. "If an engineer were building a bridge across a river, would it make sense to finance construction to get it *half way across the river?*" The banker did not get my point. The answer was "No". Other banks wouldn't even give us an appointment, so we had no options.

With a $50,000 line of credit, we struggled toward our goal to deliver 60,000 candles before Christmas, so that we could collect on this $300,000 sale.

Most of our now *formerly* homeless candlemakers had not had a real home to place a Christmas tree in for a long, long time. Fathers who'd been separated from children for years because of homelessness, alcoholism and depression worked hard to have holiday gifts for kids for the first time in several seasons. *This was a motivated group.* The giant candle manufacturing firms that we beat out on this deal had high tech automated equipment worth millions of dollars to produce hundreds of thousands of candles in a day. Our candlemakers were fighting for their very lives. They were all ready to make this work, *whatever it took.* Our happy candlemakers made every single one of the Body Shop's 60,000 candles for this first order by pouring each one from tin pitchers, *by hand!*

At first we were only producing about 1,000 candles per day. This would make delivery of the goods about one month late. There was no way that we were going to prove the corporate skeptics within the Body Shop right, that we couldn't deliver this level of volume. We stopped work and formed three **quality teams:**1.) the quality of production team 2.) the quality of packaging team and 3.) the quality of life at work team.

Every employee of Candleworks was part of at least one quality team. With innovative ideas presented by these teams, we increased production by 100%. We met our production deadline. All 60,000 candles were produced with a week to spare before the required delivery date.

One third of the 60,000 candles were sold directly to the Body Shop Corporate Warehouse to supply their company owned stores. The other two thirds were to be sold to the Body Shops operated independently by franchisees. The holiday season had an unexpected retail market slump. $60,000 dollars worth of the goods scheduled to be sold out to the franchise stores still sat on our shelves in mid-December. We had produced the volume promised to The Body Shop. With undelivered inventory, Candleworks now discovered what is old hat to old time entrepreneurs: a *cash flow crunch.*

We had developed a very open relationship with the bank officer that had originally received the "social responsibility" pitch from Wendy Germain at The Better Homes Fund. We shared with him our situation; to see if we could pry loose the other $50,000 line of credit that we'd originally demonstrated that we needed when we launched this project.

We honestly disclosed our short term cash challenge with the lending officer. He took our query to his corporate supervisors. (This bank is one of the largest interstate banking conglomerates in the U.S.) Much to our surprise, the response was a unilateral attack on the Candleworks checking account. With no notice, and with no signature from Candleworks directors, $16,000 was debited against our checking account, leaving us with only a $200 balance. Our loan was paid down *without our consent* from $50,000 to $34,000. By agreement, interest had been deducted automatically from our account. According to our loan terms, no principal was due for two more months. Later, we found out why this happened. The Better Homes Fund had changed their policy to conventional fund raising methods. They were no longer selling goods from Candleworks and several other enterprises operated by homeless families. Without a tie to their high profile corporate customer, Candleworks had no importance or value to this giant bank.

In the classic story *"A Christmas Carol"*, Tiny Tim, a little kid on crutches almost had his holiday ruined by Scrooge, a nineteenth century money-lender. At Candleworks, we had a whole room full of "Tiny Tims"; on crutches, in wheel chairs, with an array of physical, mental and circumstantial/social disabilities.

The Big Bank decided to play the role of Scrooge. Just days before Christmas, $16,000 was debited from our account *with no notice whatsoever.* Candleworks had no way to cover payroll for the Christmas Holidays. Fortunately, friends and family came forward in the true Christmas spirit and made loans to Candleworks. Employees received the money they needed for necessities and Holiday gifts for their newly re-united families. This called for celebration!

Our three quality teams were temporarily renamed and reassigned:

1. Quality of production team became the "quality of the main course" team.

2. Quality of packaging team became "quality of side dishes" team.

3. Quality of life at work team became "quality of holiday deserts" team.

We celebrated everyone's hard work with a great Holiday Feast. We invited community leaders, friends, family and our local customers to join in the party. Our three teams delivered the most sumptuous and bountiful spread of food anyone in our group had ever seen. Paychecks and bonuses were handed out and we all adjourned for a well-deserved seasonal vacation.

After Christmas, we sent out marketing letters to all of the Body Shop Franchisees to move the other $60,000 of inventory left from the Holiday shopping season. We notified The Big Bank about our plan to liquidate inventory to solve our cash flow crunch. The officer that had originally been recruited to our cause left the institution for another job. Without our informal connection to the major bank's multi-million dollar corporate customer, we were on our own. We had no conventional collateral. We had no connections. We'd been dealing with an amiable and conscientious loan officer at this big bank *person to person*. His new replacement was an impersonal corporate number cruncher shipped in from the head office in another state. The new officer refused to renew our loan. He called in the entire $34,000 balance as *due in full*. Candleworks had great business prospects. Our biggest challenge was rapid growth that required credit for more production. This new loan officer sent us a curt letter that literally stated that this large multi-state banking conglomerate *"had no interest in the growth of Candleworks"*. At a business conference, I met another entrepreneur that had started up a bootstrap business in telemarketing. The very same new officer at the same bank had also called their loan in *during the exact same month as ours*. It seemed this large commercial bank had changed their loan policy. Bootstrapping entrepreneurial ventures were not their designated market. The telemarketing firm with the bootstrap origins is now doing 100 million dollars of business this year! They are not doing any business with their old bank. *Some bootstrappers eventually become very major players*! The same year, the documentary that won the Academy Award, was about an Iowa family evicted from the farm they'd homesteaded 100 years earlier. The bank in this real life drama? -*the same giant bank*.

> *A banker is a guy that gives you an umbrella on a sunny day, and takes it away when it rains.*
> -WALT DISNEY

At this point, I fully realized that giant banking conglomerates were not the bank of choice for bootstrappers. Most bootstrap organizations don't even get in the door of a major bank. The few that do, rarely come out with the development money they need. Large commercial banks usually work with established borrowers that have a strong credit record and the safety of real estate or other collateral. This large bank was just carrying out their mission of protecting the assets of their depositors and maximixing profit. The large bank's mission and Candlework's mission simply did not match. Creative financing is a very important skill for an entrepreneur to learn. Developing a strong financial base is necessary for a social entrepreneur; *no margin, no mission!* If your bootstrap enterprise hits a barrier or encounters a major problem, don't waste energy blaming any outside source; it's *your responsibility* to find options. Convert the energy of worry and blame to creativity.

In many Muslim nations, banking law requires that banks *partner* with entrepreneurs and *share risk*. In Western nations, banks charge interest and attempt to insulate the bank from risk as much as possible. The Muslim banks only collect interest *after the enterprise becomes profitable*. Such an arrangement creates a much more involved and constructive relationship between entrepreneurs and bankers. Historically, in our own Judeo-Christian/Western tradition, interest rates collectable by lenders were also carefully controlled. A couple of decades ago, traditional *usury laws* were taken off of the law books in the U.S. In the Christian gospels, Jesus drove money lenders from the temple. If a community wants their local banks to be more socially responsible, then consumers must expect and demand this ethic. It's *our money* banks are managing, *let's develop creative new banking options.*

A community leader in our own town heard about our turn of events with the out of town "Big Bank". She set up a meeting with the commercial lending officer of a small bank *in our own community*. This loan officer said yes, he'd like to work with Candleworks. They had a direct interest in our work in the community. Lynette and I then participated in a very thorough business training course through the Entrepreneurial Center of the local College of Business Administration. This was a hands-on course in business planning sponsored by the Entrepreneurial Center set-up by the Kauffman Foundation and The University of Iowa.

The objective of the "Fast Track" entrepreneurial training program was to write a thorough business plan. At Fast Track, Candleworks had the good fortune of working with Jim Daily, a very talented M.B.A. candidate. Jim had operated his own business before returning to graduate school. Together, we measured labor costs on each candle type that we manufactured. We calculated the cost of all raw materials down to the penny. We projected all of our general overhead costs for a one year cycle. We were able to be very accurate in projecting revenue, because we already had major purchase orders in hand. Our M.B.A. intern worked with us to create our own specialized industry computer program to track our production schedules, cash-flow, and inventory. We did our homework.

To produce all of the goods that we had already sold, Candleworks needed an operating line of credit of $300,000. We presented all of our well researched and documented data to our local commercial lending officer. He had first visited us when we were operating as a small workshop with just a few employees. Now he was visiting us in a full size factory building in our community's industrial park with over 50 employees. Bankers tend to be conservative. Candleworks was entrepreneurial, growing, and highly innovative. We operate with a new social and economic paradigm. His initial interest was now tempered with caution.

Fall arrived. Candleworks was gearing up to produce literally hundreds of thousands of candles in just a few weeks to supply all of our customers with products for the holiday retail rush. We were living hand to mouth, *still without an operating line of credit.*

I now have a new definition of reality; facing 50 people on each Friday who need their paycheck. Sometimes on Thursday, I wouldn't know exactly where the cash would be collected from. Some weeks we operated by sheer Divine Providence. We'd need $8,000 for payroll for Friday afternoon. On Friday morning $8,050 in checks would arrive at our post office box from customers all over the country. An entrepreneur by nature and necessity lives by faith. Cutting it this close though is living on the edge. A few weeks, we fell over the edge and we had no cash to operate. In these situations, I'd sit down with all the candlemakers and honestly share our situation. Everyone bonded together. We worked on through each cash crunch. We faced all challenges as a team.

At this point, Candleworks was approached by a factoring agent. Factors are a sometimes necessary, yet very expensive alternative to conventional bank financing. After a manufacturer like Candleworks ships out a truck load of goods, we then wait 30 to 60 days to finally get paid. A factor closes this time gap by purchasing invoices on delivered goods for an 8% discount on the gross amount of the invoice. Eight percent for two months use of funds is equivalent to 48% annual interest! When you're facing the abyss, sometimes you've gotta dance with the devil.

We financed the busiest season of our existence by factoring our invoices. By factoring, we basically gave away our profit for that season, so that we could continue to exist and keep the 50 jobs we'd created alive. The bank was still reviewing our S.B.A. forms.

At the beginning of November, I presented an alternate plan to our local bank; why not assign our major corporate invoices to the bank instead of to a factoring agent? Our customers would then remit their payment *directly* to the bank and pay back on a revolving line of credit. Our corporate customers were highly credit worthy: Matrix/Biolage is a division of Bristol Meyer. The Body Shop is a global retail giant.

Candleworks assigned two large invoices that totaled $125,000 from The Body Shop and Biolage/Matrix. We were thus able to provide operating cash with the convenience of a factor, without the exorbitant cost.

Our bank charged us conventional bank interest rates. Within 2 months we paid off the entire $125,000. Now we finance Candleworks through this method with a short-term, $250,000 line of credit. We work with a small town bank that's very responsive to our needs.

With our rapid growth, this line of credit does not provide a wide margin of operating cash. Candleworks is by necessity and design a lean, mean operation. We continue to build our manufacturing process systems out of salvaged and recycled components. Our family still lives the austere lifestyle of the bootstrapping entrepreneur. We measure success each day as we ship out quality candles to our customers. We measure our progress toward our company objectives week by week as we hand out paychecks to a group of very dedicated, hard working employees. This is the real American Way. Candleworks demonstrates the spirit of free enterprise in the raw.

DISCUSSION WITH AN ELDERLY, SUCCESSFUL ENTREPRENEUR:

Q. *"To build a successful venture, which is most important; knowledge, capital, or desire?"*

A. *"Desire. If you have **desire**, you will learn what you must and not quit until you raise the capital."*

THE EQUATION OF ENTREPRENEURIAL ENERGY:

$$\text{Vision} - \text{Effort} = \text{Fantasy}$$
$$\text{Effort} - \text{Vision} = \text{Drudgery}$$
$$\text{Vision} + \text{Effort} = \text{Success}$$

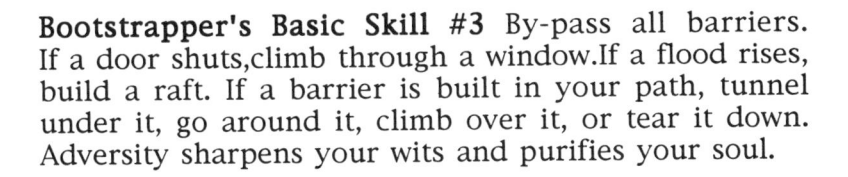

Bootstrapper's Basic Skill #3 By-pass all barriers. If a door shuts, climb through a window. If a flood rises, build a raft. If a barrier is built in your path, tunnel under it, go around it, climb over it, or tear it down. Adversity sharpens your wits and purifies your soul.

Readers notes:

What is the greatest barrier in the way of your goal?

What steps can you take to eliminate these barriers?

How do you create your own barriers by self-sabotage?

How do we assist children to learn perseverance?

Chapter Four
Getting in on the Ground Floor, and Sleeping on it too!

We leased our first permanent work space to grow Candleworks as a viable manufacturing company in March of 1994. This building was a tiny 1890's cottage near the Iowa City central business district. We began to build our business from the ground up, *literally*. We started in the cellar! And a dark, dingy little cellar at that. One way you can make sure that you get in on the "ground floor" of a business opportunity is to build it *from the bottom up,* yourself. This is the essence of entrepreneurial bootstrapping. The Richards family not only got in on the "ground floor" of this opportunity, we *slept on it too!* For the first four months of this fledgling enterprise, our family slept on the floor of the candle workshop. We did not have money for both a home and a workshop.

In the commercial development of our nation, there are countless stories of penniless immigrants coming to build the American Dream with nothing but their dream, close knit families and hard work. Candleworks was launched on the Lower East Side of New York. This neighborhood has a very long tradition as a place where such immigrants have settled and struggled.

In the early years of this century, Eastern Europeans crammed huge families into tiny tenements after being processed through Ellis Island in New York Harbor in the shadow of The Statue of Liberty. Now Jamaican, Latino and Asian immigrants fill the same neighborhood. Often when immigrant families set out to pursue their dream, a father and son or a couple of brothers forge ahead to the "New World", to lay the foundation of a new entrepreneurial enterprise. After they have the business up and running, wives, children, cousins, aunts and uncles follow to build the business as it grows. The U.S. economy has grown into the greatest in the world in this way. Bootstrapping is at the very foundation of our country's political and economic democracy.

After our start-up in New York City, our family sent our son, Solomon, and I ahead to Iowa to build the foundation of Candleworks. Our son, Mel, stayed with Lynette in New York as she held down her job to keep transitional income coming in during this move. Our oldest son, Michael remained at New York University to continue work on his neuroscience degree. Our other son, Ben was in L.A. following up on his movie deal with Warner Brothers.

We paid our first month of rent on our building in Iowa and ordered the initial deliveries of raw materials for the business. There was very little money left for personal needs. Solomon and I slept on the ground floor of the candle workshop in sleeping bags. We worked long hours, so sleep came easy, even though our accommodations were definitely "ground floor".

This old house had a basement filled with several years of debris left behind by a parade of previous tenants who'd attempted to start small businesses, gave up and moved on. Seven out of ten new businesses do not survive more that a year or two. Bootstrapping is not for the timid. Courage and perseverance are required.

We still kept our first company vehicle, the two wheel hand-truck to move materials inside our workshop. We added our first motorized company vehicle; a rusty old Ford van. We loaded up all the junk from the basement and made multiple trips to the county solid waste dump. After we had achieved clean, empty space in the basement, we set out to convert the dreary cellar into a cheery candle crafting workshop.

First we painted every wall a light, very subdued celery green. Now it was time to furnish and equip our first space that was dedicated solely as a candle making workshop. All of our past work had been in temporary facilities. Our homeless enterprise finally had a home.

I went to the homeless shelter 6 blocks away and recruited the first two Candleworks employees. Larry and John introduced me to the fine art of "dumpster diving". Dumpster diving is a very important survival skill learned by many homeless people in shelters and on the streets. An accomplished dumpster diver enjoys high esteem and status in the homeless community. When you have no cash or employment, dumpster diving is one of the few ways available to acquire the things you need and desire.

Since Iowa City has a very large state university, May is the prime-time for dumpster diving. Graduating students are moving to far off cities to launch careers. They find it more costly and inconvenient to move furniture and other possessions than to replace them at their new home destination. Larry and John started hauling in window fans, tables, workbenches, desks, chairs and a wide variety of lighting fixtures for our workshop. Our entire facility was equipped and furnished with items from these dumpster diving forays. We built all of our workshop fixtures with wood found in construction dumpsters.

Within a couple of weeks, we had all the warehouse shelving, workshop and office furnishings that we needed to launch the business. The only new items we purchased were a fax machine and a computer. Even our phones had been salvaged from successful dumpster hauls. On the day that we were ready to actually start making our first candles, John hauled in a functional FM Radio/Stereo from a dumpster down the block. The first candles were made by happy people singing along to the "golden oldies" station.

We hired one more guy named John and another referral from the homeless shelter, August. We had a hard working crew who realized that this job was both enjoyable and financially productive. After a few days of work, August asked if he could borrow the old company van after work. I checked his driver's license and gave him the keys. The next morning we all came to work to find the entrance to our candle workshop blocked by huge piles of pine lumber.

August had spent the night before loading up the van with a bountiful dumpster retrieval; thousands of board feet of pine boards had been used for protective crating around new windows being installed at one of the large university student residence buildings. John and Larry designed a prototype pine counter top display unit for our customers to effectively market our candles in their retail stores. I then wrote up a promotional letter that offered a complimentary point of sale display unit to any customer that ordered a minimum $200 candle order that week. *The orders poured in.* John, Larry and August made over one hundred pine display units. We shipped candle orders and hand crafted wooden display units to customers all over the United States and Canada.

Iowa City has a lot of people living on the street. The homeless shelter has an enforced maximum stay of several weeks because of limited space. Larry and John's shelter time ran out before they had saved up enough money from their new jobs to rent a permanent apartment. They moved into the attic above the Candle Workshop. A few more days of dumpster diving provided them with all the comforts of home; *their first home in years.*

Now that Candleworks has bootstrapped our way up from a tiny, dark cellar into a 10,000 square foot manufacturing facility in an industrial park, we've moved beyond dumpster diving. The *waste not, want not* ethic that was there in the beginning is still a foundation principle of our business operation. Nothing is wasted. We scrape up all waste wax on the floor to create a novel secondary product; fireplace starters made from scrap wax and saw dust. We package our goods for shipment in recycled materials. We continue to expand and build our plant with recycled components from salvage sources. One of the mottoes of Candleworks is *"We recycle materials and rebuild lives."*

During our first summer in Iowa, we hired a few more people from the Emergency Housing Shelter. Orders were rolling in. We had a posted starting time for the work day of 8:30 a.m. Since I was sleeping on the floor of the Candle Workshop, I'd be up early to prepare for the day. Knocks would come earlier and earlier from homeless candlemakers who were eager to get busy. Eight o'clock, seven-thirty. The myth that people were on the street because they were too lazy to work was proven *very wrong*. Our candlemakers would compete with each other to see who would get there first to retrieve orders from the fax machine. They'd eagerly plan out the colors, quantities and sizes of candles that we'd need to produce that day. No one who worked with us remained homeless for more than a few weeks. Candleworks provided interest free loans for rent and deposits to get our people into permanent housing. Everyone worked together to find furnishings, and help new people move. We created a business to provide jobs and a community of mutual support to meet other essential needs.

Work is one of the most important essential human needs. When this need is met, people are nurtured in very important ways. The old welfare paradigm damages self-worth. Economic self-reliance boosts it. An important demonstration of social science was taking place in the humble, yet happy surroundings of Candleworks. More newspapers came to write stories about this phenomenon. Local and national television news crews showed up at our door to do reports. A few college professors took an interest in observing our real life laboratory of labor and life. We were putting Candleworks on the map!

The very basis of society is human participation in the endless cycle of giving and receiving: goods, care, information, knowledge. People thrive when they actively participate in this vital interchange. People are damaged psychologically and emotionally when such participation is absent. Social isolation creates social aberration. Consider the case of the "Unibomber". His extreme isolation led to his terrorist acts.

Larry and John, both very serious street alcoholics, quit drinking *of their own volition* in this stimulating environment. August had been asked to leave the homeless shelter because of persistent behavioral problems. He made progress in this new environment. People who ran neighboring businesses began to notice these personal transformations of Candleworks participants. The homeless shelter, and social service agencies sent us their most difficult cases.

Several independent nominations were simultaneously presented to The City Human Rights Commission to cite Candleworks for these innovative efforts. Just six months after we set up shop in Iowa City, the Human Rights Commission named Candleworks "BUSINESS OF THE YEAR". The award was presented by the director of the homeless shelter at an awards banquet of business, government and university leaders.

TEXT OF THE ACCEPTANCE SPEECH BY MICHAEL RICHARDS AT THIS AWARDS PRESENTATION:

"All the Candlemakers accept this award with gratitude. We accept this award with some sadness, however. Why should it be, that Candleworks, a small business that has been in this community for only six months be selected for this award? Why wouldn't businesses that have been a part of this community for years and even decades be recognized for providing

these kinds of job opportunities for disadvantaged and disabled persons in our community? The kind of opportunities and jobs that Candleworks creates for people in need could be so common as to not even be noticed.

If all businesses created a few jobs for disadvantaged and disabled persons, we could actually eliminate poverty and despair in this one community. This community could then serve as a model to communities all over the U.S. We could demonstrate how to create community wealth and not just corporate wealth.

Candleworks will provide a training setting for any business here this morning that wishes to hire people from the homeless shelter or other people with disadvantages and disabilities. Workers can train for several weeks with our Candlemakers to learn punctual job attendance, quality task performance and team participation. Then they can transfer to other businesses in this community so our effort can multiply."

Everyone applauded, but they quickly left the breakfast to get back to business as usual. John, a severely disabled homeless man who accepted the award with me commented: *"Everyone just kept munchin' down on their breakfast during your talk, like their meal was all that mattered."* This offer and challenge to area businesses was first presented several years ago. This statement has been reiterated on several news broadcasts. It has been re-printed in several area newspaper articles. *Thus far, not one business has accepted this challenge.* Why?

Whether businesses calculate social costs such as crime, drug abuse and homelessness into the profit and loss statements of their companies, these costs exist. These costs directly affect their businesses and the community. These costs are assumed *inefficiently* through large government structures that then charge back this "social overhead" in the form of high local, state and federal taxes. *That system doesn't work.* It costs about fifty thousand dollars a year to lock up our social casualties in prison. The average prison sentence is 7 years. $350,000 for each prisoner! A lot of bootstrap businesses could start with this misused cash!

Businesses need to become more proactive, and plan these social costs into their business strategy. A business operates in a community, not in a vacuum. The resources of business could be put to work to create new models of social entrepreneurship. These social costs could actually be *decreased dramatically.* Candleworks models this social entrepreneurship. Now communities all over the U.S. and Europe are seeking our assistance and consulting to replicate this model. For information on consulting, call: **319-354-7515.**

Welfare reform will begin to bring this realization to the fore. Last year, there was an insightful cartoon on the front page of the *Des Moines Sunday Register*; this cartoon caricatured our conservative governor, Terrence Branstad at a national trade fair promoting Iowa Business. *The sign on his information booth states:*

"IOWA ECONOMIC DEVELOPMENT:
PIGS, PRISONS AND POKER"

The largest economic development efforts in our state have been gambling, prisons and pork processing plants. *Something is seriously wrong with this picture.* Because of the tradition of Iowa's strong agricultural economy, this state has become very complacent in regard to entrepreneurial economic development of alternative industry and enterprise. A Washington D.C. based think-tank recently rated all 50 states for entrepreneurial activity and climate. Iowa was ranked last at # 50! Candleworks is like an oasis in a dry desert.

The premise that building new prisons will create jobs and economic expansion is evidence of a serious social sickness. When you consider the racial statistics on prison population, it is also a symptom of deep rooted racism. Most prisons have more than 50% black population. Housing prisoners for long periods of time is much more costly than preventative measures. We need to create education, employment training and economic development for youth, minorities and disadvantaged groups, *via the Candleworks model.*

To tout gambling enterprises as the centerpiece of our state's economic development is myopic to the extreme. Iowa's many gambling enterprises have brought very little new money into the state. Gambling simply *redistributes* the scarce economic resources of poor and middle class people into the hands of a few exploitive corporations that run the casino scam. These corporations are totally devoid of social responsibility. They add no value to the economy. Divorce, alcoholism, even suicide have grown dramatically in states that have bought the *get rich quick lie* of commercial gambling enterprises. The small gain in tax revenues are quickly consumed with the higher social costs that gambling creates. *It's time to wake up and think.* If state governments re-directed the efforts that promote more prisons and poker into effective social entrepreneurship, we could start solving problems.

I am an entrepreneur with a free-market, even libertarian attitude about society and commerce. I am not suggesting that gambling be outlawed. But for *government* to promote gambling as community economic development is a sad lie and a reflection of the lack of intelligence and vision of many state legislators. *The blind are leading the blind.* Visionary entrepreneurs are urgently needed to build a new society.

At Candleworks, we've assisted several casualties of compulsive gambling to reconstruct their lives after they bought the false hope of un-earned instant wealth. Their gambling led to alcohol and drug abuse, crime, divorce, depression and homelessness. They're now working with us, putting their life back together one step at a time. They're playing life's *real game* again.

Just as our candlemaking crew was coalescing as a functional, efficient work group, we received very challenging news. The Body Shop, our major customer, and thus our primary source of income and jobs, put our candle products on hiatus. A new group of corporate managers were deciding if our candles would continue to be part of The Body Shop's new retail product plan.

This hiatus lasted several extremely difficult months. During this time, Candleworks made very few sales and generated very little income. At this point, I was sleeping on the floor of our tiny candle workshop. Our formerly homeless work group were living in temporary quarters in the attic. Everyone decided to stick it out together and *work through this adversity*. We all kept our humor and joy alive. I got busy looking for new customers for our hand made candles.

We re-directed the time that we'd been using to make thousands of Body Shop candles to improve our work environment. We painted our humble little workshop building, inside and out. We planted flower gardens. One emotionally vulnerable young man wandered over from the homeless shelter. He loved everyone's enthusiasm. *He asked for a paint brush to help.* All the candlemakers encouraged him to move in and help build Candleworks. He decided he couldn't wait several months for Candleworks to find new customers so we could hire him. He jumped on a Greyhound bus. The bus stopped for a cafe stop on the Illinois border. He called home to his family in Indiana. They told him not to bother coming back home. He felt trapped and without options. He never got back on the bus. He shot himself in the head. *He'd just given up on life.*

With this disturbing news, a room full of grieving candlemakers worked in determined silence. We realized how totally dependent Candleworks had been on just one customer. This caused us to evaluate how vulnerable we were to the decisions of outside organizations. We could not let the future of our people rest in the hands of executives in distant corporate offices. They did not feel what we felt each day. We could not expect them to take responsibility for us, *that was our responsibility.* We made a commitment to build a stronger base. In our present situation we had no way to operate with *autonomy* and *security*. The main desire of an entrepreneur is autonomy and self-determination. *We needed a much wider customer base.*

It was as if the weakness of our fallen friend had caused a great rise of new strength in the survivors. All the candlemakers deepened our firm bond of commitment. I set out to diversify and expand our customer base. Twenty miles away from our candle workshop in the tiny village of Norway, Iowa was the largest distributor of herbal teas and organic coffees in the world, Frontier Co-op. Frontier is a consumer's co-operative that is owned by more than seven thousand member food co-ops and natural food stores. Frontier products are marketed through a product catalog that is sent out to all 7,000 wholesale members, and also to thousands of non-member retail customers. Frontier had expanded their product base to other natural food products, health supplements and related natural products and accessories. I set up a meeting with Frontier's purchasing manager. Within one month, all of the various products hand-crafted by Candleworks were listed in the accessory section of the Frontier catalog. Our work was marketed to thousands of new customers. *This was a lifesaver.*

The initial customer response from Frontier Co-op only brought in about 25% of the sales volume we had been receiving regularly from The Body Shop retail group. However, this provided survival revenue for

Candleworks and survival income for our small band of merry candlemakers. Frontier's large customer base would provide great long-term opportunities for further growth of Candleworks. This convinced me that the long term health of Candleworks required further diversification of our market base. *I got busy.*

The world must have *known* we were ready for new customers. A call came in to us from Vermont. The buying manager for Ben and Jerry's Ice Cream Empire wanted to know if we could create candles with their trade mark black and white Jersey cow spots. Candleworks was ready to try anything to keep these jobs viable. We found small terra-cotta pots, painted them white, and added the black spots. We put a wick in each clay pot and filled them with scented wax. How do you scent a cow candle? The largest tourist attraction in the entire state of Vermont is the Ben and Jerry's Ice Cream Factory. A gift shop had been added to their plant to accommodate the flood of visitors. Our candles were added to their gift shop.

Next, my son, Benjamin called from California. He had spotted rolled beeswax candles like the ones Candleworks made in the Santa Monica location of Urban Outfitters. Urban Outfitters is one of America's most creative retailers. They sell fashionable clothing, tapes and CD's, contemporary furniture, creative housewares, etc. Every Urban Outfitters store is a stimulating open space, post-modern, de-constructed urban/industrial environment. Urban Outfitters is the new-wave department store for Generation X. They have about twenty locations, all in the most trendy settings in urban America: New York's Greenwich Village and Soho, California's Santa Monica Pedestrian Mall, Chicago's Clark street, etc.

I got through for a direct phone conversation with Urban Outfitters head housewares buyer; *on the very day they had decided to discontinue selling rolled beeswax candles!* Urban Outfitters offers a real hands-on, participatory shopping experience. It seems their lively customers were squeezing the candles as they picked them up for inspection. Candles that were not purchased quickly took on a pinched, less than perfect quality. I received a courteous, even interested listen from the buyer about the origins and work of Candleworks. I also received a very succinct "no" about trying beeswax candles from us as a new source. This "no" almost led to a quick click and dial tone on the other end. I almost felt myself reach out across the phone line to hold on, I said: "Please, don't hang up".

I then asked, "If you don't need beeswax candles, what are you interested in as a new product?" The Urban Outfitters buyer described to me a common recycled tin can, cut with a propane torch to create a tin lantern for a votive candle. Urban Outfitters had already found a place to have these produced for their stores in Mexico. If Candleworks could create the same product for the same "third-world" price, we could have the job. This was a great thing for a bootstrapper to learn: *If a customer doesn't want to buy what you make; then make for them what they want to buy.*

We couldn't safely set up a cutting torch inside the apartments where candlemakers worked in New York City or the converted house we worked in Iowa. Urban Outfitters sent us a sample of this creative product. All we needed now was a place to make this new item. Lynette's brother, Owen is an Iowa farmer. Like many farmers, he has welding equipment and cutting torches to maintain and alter farm equipment in his self-sufficient workshop. We sent the prototype from Urban Outfitters to his farm. He went to the county recycling center in a nearby town and got a bag of old soup and fruit cans to practice on. Within a few hours, Owen created a candle lantern comparable to the one sent to us by Urban Outfitters. A homeless woman apprenticed on the cutting torch. She found a new career, a new purpose and a new life. We expanded our line of candle accessory products made from recycled tin cans. CBS THIS MORNING, sent a camera crew out from New York. Our bootstrapping story about *"creating something from nothing"* was broadcast to a national news audience. Calls poured in. The Body Shop national headquarters then sent us a formal letter, re-instating Candleworks as a vendor. They added several new candle colors that matched the color pallet of other Body Shop products. They sent the new order form via a national "blast fax" to all store locations. The next morning, eager candlemakers arrived in the office at about seven-fifteen and let out hoots of joy; the fax machine had spun out order after order all across the entire office floor! Now everyone was getting their first taste of job-security. It was a new emotion to feel needed and productive. The effect of newly claimed self-esteem was evident in sober mornings, clean clothes, big bright smiles, better grooming and positive attitudes.

We realized that our niche in the marketplace was to create custom made, private label candle products. We made novelty candles for Ben and Jerry's, vegetable wax candles for The Body Shop and creative recycled tin candle accessories for Urban Outfitters. This custom product development is still our present approach to marketing and manufacturing. We now continue to expand our national customer base through assertive "guerrilla marketing". We find out who can make a purchasing decision for a chain of stores, and continue direct contact with them until we get a deal.

Bootstrapper's Basic Skill #4: Accept deferred gratification. In the early development of making your dream a reality, accept the *joy* of your work as your main pay. Outer rewards of financial freedom, maybe even fame, will come your way if you persevere. When these external rewards do come, they will never have as great of a value as the original joy and satisfaction derived from pursuing your dream against all odds. The primary reward for work well done is simply more work. Let your work be your joy.

Chapter Five
The Entrepreneurial Soup
Late Night Experiments

If you're launching your bootstrap enterprise so that you won't have to work as hard as you do at your present job, you're barking up the wrong tree. Entrepreneurs work 16 hour days so that they can escape an 8 hour day! The difference is that you *own all 24 of your hours.* Independence and self-determination are the main motivators of most entrepreneurs, not just money.

The major breakthroughs in new products, new plans for innovative marketing for Candleworks usually take place at 2 or 3 in the morning, *while normal working people are resting up from their 8 hour work days.* Expect to spend 8 hours a day running the day to day operation of your enterprise. Your overtime is spent stirring up your creative entrepreneurial soup.

Your 8 hour days are spent serving up the regular menu. A Master Chef creates the creative cuisine *after hours* to add magic for the next day's house specials. The bootstrapper spends 8 hours a day just to insure that their enterprise will *survive.* After hours is when you hatch the ideas and plans that allow you to *thrive.*

Don't hesitate to cook up something that no one has ever tried before. Bootstrappers leap in where angels and work-a-day salarymen fear to tread. Innovate!

In the book, *The History of Scientific Revolutions*, a core premise is that most great human advancements happen by "amateurs" in a given field. These scientific innovators may very well be accomplished professionals in *another field*, but where they make their entrepreneurial breakthrough is by crossing a fence and plowing up new ground. The unconditioned point of view of an amateur allows them to "think outside of the box" and create a new paradigm. Candleworks was built by amateurs who had the raw courage to just start, to work, and learn. We've gradually gained expertise in our field. Common sense and sweat equity were our primary resources.

> *Common sense is genius dressed in work clothes."*
> -RALPH WALDO EMERSON

The Body Shop is a giant multi-national company with 1200 retail outlets in dozens of nations. In a well equipped high tech laboratory in England in 1993, their research and development chemists worked to create a novel vegetable base wax for The Body Shop's new line of natural wax aromatherapy candles.

Half way around the world, in a dimly lit kitchen in a rural homesteader's cabin, a family of transplanted New York urban homesteaders were cooking up some entrepreneurial soup: a *unique new formula for vegetable wax candles.* The Body Shop wanted to provide their customers with a natural alternative to the animal and petroleum by-product wax candles that were sold in most stores around the world. We were determined to make it happen in our late night makeshift laboratory in our tiny kitchen.

In more that a dozen other well-equipped facilities in locations in several countries, professional chemists employed by the largest candle manufacturing companies in the world, joined in the competition to create this natural wax product for The Body Shop.

Against all odds, Candleworks created the best vegetable wax formula in the kitchen of our little cabin! Our undercapitalized team of bootstrappers got the big deal! Our new line of "Body Shop" vegetable wax candle products provided the opportunity for our sales to grow by one hundred percent in our first year of operations in Iowa. Candleworks had been named "Business of the Year" by the Human Rights Commission of our City Government. The Iowa City Community Development Office then sponsored a $50,000 economic development grant. These funds provided an electronic liquid filler system, so that we could meet the demands for increased production for The Body Shop deal and create more jobs. In our second year, sales grew to six hundred thousand dollars of sales. Since conventional sources of development capital are not yet available to Candleworks, *we've purposefully moderated the pace of our growth.* In our third year, our sales again grew dramatically, creating sales of almost one million dollars.

We realized that the vegetable wax that we had developed for The Body Shop could be our key to *set ourselves apart* in the very competitive candle manufacturing industry. Our first formula for vegetable wax candles included sweet almond oil imported from Italy and vegetable waxes derived from tropical plants imported from various sources in Latin America. This formula cost more than 3 times the cost of traditional paraffin based candle waxes. We now needed to create a vegetable based candle wax that was cost competitive with petroleum based paraffin waxes.

Sometimes the key to finding the best idea for a creative enterprise is to look right under your nose. Candleworks is located in Iowa, right in the heart of the most bountiful soy bean producing area in the world. Why not make candles from *soy bean oil?*

I am not a chemist, but I have a very good mind for step by step logic and trial and error problem solving. I started the process of developing a soy oil based candle through creative thinking and methodical material testing.

Here's how we proceeded:

1. 100%, 150 degree melt-point hydrogenated soy oil was too hard.
2. try 90% hydrogenated soy, and add in non-hydrogenated soy oil to create a softer wax.
3. some cracking of the wax surface, we'll try a variety of plant based additives to create a smooth surface; glycerin, coconut oil, etc. etc.

<u>We kept a log book of every step in this process:</u>

15% of this, 75 % of that, 10% of another additive. candle burns well, wax still cracks.

20% of this, 75 % of that, 5% of another additive; candle burns well, wax now has a more consistent surface.

This process went on for more than 30 rounds of testing, until we created an ideal formula for our soy bean based candle. Our innovative soy candle burns clean. The wax surface is smooth and even. It carries fragrance scent oils very well. It's very cost effective.

This wax was created with soy beans grown in our own back yard, rather than made with costly materials imported from around the world. Our innovative candle is a value-added product of Iowa's agricultural economy. Our vegetable wax now costs the same as petroleum based paraffin wax. Now we were ready to jump into the natural products market aggressively.

Entrepreneurial success does not always require the invention of a high tech marvel. Perhaps just a better mousetrap, or in our case, *a new formula for candle wax* will bring success. A candle is a comparatively simple product to manufacture. Candles are one of the oldest consumer products in the history of commerce. Nevertheless, we created a novel new product, and thus developed an expanding new global market.

Our next step was to take our new natural wax candle products to the Natural Products Expo. This is the world's largest trade show for the natural products industry. The Fall session of the Expo always takes place on the East Coast and the Spring session takes place on the West Coast. Here, we had the opportunity to present our innovative new candle wax to thousands of potential customers in the international natural products market.

One of our first customers for our soy bean, home grown candle was, Aura Cacia, a giant in this industry. At the Expo we started negotiating a private label candlemaking agreement with Wild Oats, a chain of Natural Food Markets based in Boulder, Colorado.

You can't taste the entrepreneurial soup with a dainty teaspoon, you've gotta' dive into the kettle head first and take a big healthy slurp. If you can't take the heat, don't come into the kitchen. A bootstrapping entrepreneur wades into their chosen field, rolls up their sleeves and gets their hands dirty. Whatever your field of endeavor, *total immersion* is the key to bootstrapping your way to success; if you're a farmer, developing a new breed of cattle, you'll be wading to the top of your boots in cow manure. If you are a cabinetmaker, creating new furniture designs, your world will be mountains of sawdust. If you are publishing a new magazine, you'll be working around the clock with printer's ink smudged on your face. In our case, creating a candle manufacturing plant, I have not owned one pair of shoes that were not covered with wax for years! If you want to leave footprints in the sands of time, *wear work boots!*

Total commitment is the price of admission to the community of entrepreneurs. Commitment generates power and energy. Commitment creates enthusiasm. You can only make a commitment to a person, a cause or a career that you care deeply about. Care is the root of courage. No one ever carried out a courageous act for something they were indifferent about. Courage will create the will to persevere through challenges.

> *Until one is committed there is hesitancy, the chance to draw back... always ineffectiveness. Concerning all acts of initiative and creation there is one elementary truth, the ignorance of which kills countless ideas and splendid plans: that the moment one definitely commits oneself to move into action, then Providence moves too. All sorts of things occur to help one that would never otherwise have occurred. A whole stream of events issues from the decision, raising in one's favor all manner of unforeseen incidents and meetings and material assistance, which no one could have dreamt would have come his way.*
> —W.H. MURRAY

A folk wisdom says it all: *"In regards to ham and eggs, the chicken is participating, but the pig is committed."*

Bootstrapper's Basic Skill #5: Make a whole hearted commitment. Without the passion of total enthusiastic commitment, you won't have the energy to transform your dream into reality. Commitment creates energy. Commitment and care build courage.

Reader's notes:

What have I demonstrated the strongest commitment to thus far in my life?

What is the "passion center" of my life now?

What action steps can I take to transform my passion center into my profit center?

Chapter Six
Dumpster Diving: Recycling Undervalued Lives, Used Materials and Old Machines

Synergy is a very important operating principle of Candleworks. Synergy is a process where the whole becomes much greater than the sum of the parts. Candleworks strives for a vital new synergy of people, material and ideas. We have taken many parts that had been thrown away by other segments of society to build a whole system that is very valuable.

The most important resource that we reclaim and re-organize are people that society has thrown away. In the U.S., 75% of all disabled and disadvantaged people are left out of the job market and are chronically unemployed. 100% of the workers at Candleworks have come from these cast-off segments of society. There is no greater waste in modern culture than the waste of human potential at all levels. At Candleworks, we stop this trend in it's tracks and start a new trend.

Candleworks has been built by recycling resources. We actually developed our first manufacturing system in a building that we recycled. This building was literally a shack along the muddy banks of the Iowa River. This structure had been abandoned during the devastating 1993 floods along the Mississippi River Valley (the Iowa River is major a tributary that flows directly into the Mississippi). After the floods, this shack was filled with tons of mud and flood debris. To reclaim it for use, we hauled out three dump trucks full of mud, tin cans,bottles,garbage and rusted out hulks of old stoves, freezers and other abandoned appliances.

In this makeshift factory, we started making the gift baskets with our candles and Cape Cod Work's soaps for the Better Homes Fund's Mother's Day fund raising premium gift. Wendy Germain of the Better Homes Fund had been working on a project with Jackson and Perkins, the famous rose garden mail order catalog. At the request of Wendy, Jackson and Perkins shipped one hundred rose bushes that they donated to Candleworks. Wendy flew out from Boston, and took up a shovel with all the candlemakers. At first, skeptical neighbors near the abandoned shack wondered what would happen if a group of homeless people moved into their neighborhood. They found out! We converted a shack and a junk-yard into a showplace on the river surrounded by rose gardens. All summer long, our neighbors came and clipped rose bouquets to take back home. Candleworks is about making candles, creating jobs, building community. *Business has a larger context than just the bottom line.*

All of our neighbors continued to come and visit, *except one.* The one neighbor that never came to pick a rose called the County Board of Supervisors. She told them that Candleworks had brought "dangerous people" to her neighborhood. She insisted that they close us down because our little shack was not zoned for business. The Board forced us out of the building. We set out looking for a new home. Steve Long, one of the staff in the City Planning Office heard about the situation. He came with another City colleague, Steve Nasby to visit our humble shop. They then worked with Candleworks to apply for Community Economic Development funds to get our fledgling bootstrap enterprise onto more solid financial ground.

Our first candle making equipment was created from salvaged industrial components and scrap materials. One wonderful piece of gerry-rigged equipment we dubbed the "Wick Wacker". The "Wick Wacker" had a grooved rod hooked up to a rotary drill to provide motive power. This Rube Goldberg piece of equipment wound up wick around the grooved rod. A blade then slipped down through the groove in the rod and produced hundreds of pre-measured wicks. Each wick was the length of the circumference of the rod. To create wick of various sizes, we would just insert grooved rods with a different circumference into the "Wick-Wacker". Before this innovation, each wick had been individually measured and cut by hand. The "Wick-Wacker" speeded up our wick production process one hundred-fold.

After the success of the "Wick-Wacker", we created a cousin contraption: "The Wick-Waxer". For container candles, it's necessary to pre-wax wick and insert it into a metal clip to make it stand upright in the container. The container is then filled up with molten candle wax. The "Wick Waxer" operated by moving the same rotary drill that powered the "Wick Wacker" into a slot where it turned a reel that pulled wick through a vat of molten wax and wrapped it up around another reel. We've become experts in "low-tech" manufacturing processes. Necessity is indeed the mother of invention. A bootstrapper does not have the funds for expensive state of the art equipment. Bootstrapping is the lively art of invention and improvisation. Bootstrapping requires creativity, resourcefulness, and a playful inventiveness.

After we received our first order for tens of thousands of container candles from one national chain of retail stores, one of their direct competitors contacted us to make candles for their chain of 100 stores also. We wanted products for each of these customers to have a distinctive look. We proposed a new line of pillar candles to the new customer. The only problem was, we did not own one single mold to make pillar candles!

The first chain of stores had sent us several plastic bottles of their company's various scented shampoos so that we could match the scent of their new frosted glass container candles to the scents already used in their products. After we matched up the scent, we emptied the shampoos into other containers and gave them to new employees just getting out of the local homeless shelter. Some were really ready for a fragrant shower! We then cut the top off of these plastic shampoo cylinders, and voila! -*plastic candle molds* to make the samples for pillar candles for the new customer! We literally recycled old containers of one customer to mold the prototype candles for one of their *prime competitors*. That's some ballsy recycling!

This market breakthrough was accomplished before Candleworks owned a single candle mold! The three recycled plastic cylinders were used just once to create the prototypes. These three prototypes were presented to the head buying agent of this new customer. Our prototypes were considered along with prototypes from a dozen of the largest candle manufacturers in the world, including two from Asia. Candleworks got the deal. We then convinced the new customer to pay us an advance deposit on their first order of ten thousand candles. This provided us with the capital to buy several hundred professionally crafted metal candle molds to manufacture their order. That's real bootstrapping! We created *something* from *nothing*.

Our pillar candle making has now expanded to a demand of thousands and thousands of pillar candles every year. Our most recent customer for pillar candles is the noted New York fashion designer, Eileen Fisher. We are making a special line of holiday candles for her company. We've now built our own sophisticated candle molding system. Circulating water is pumped through a room full of re-cycled galvanized tin troughs that serve as cooling tanks for our candle molds. We cool all of the circulating water in a 400 gallon stainless steel refrigerated water chiller that we recycled from a dairy farm that closed down in the county just south of the Candleworks plant. We even recycle the water through our mold cooling system.

Candleworks has grown into a major manufacturer, making hundreds of thousands of candles. We've gradually built up our manufacturing processing system out of recycled salvage components. Each day we melt tons of wax in giant steam-jacket kettles that had once been used in the food and soap industries. We converted old wagon wheels that were hauled out of a farm field into turning carousels that hold our dipping racks for taper candle making. All of our candle molds are steam cleaned in a giant old bun warming cabinet that we bought for $5 from a bakery that was going out of business. While at the bakery auction, we discovered the perfect transport system to move our candles from one production department to the next. We now have about 20 recycled bakery wheel carts to move our products around the factory. We have built and equipped our entire production plant with materials and components that had been cast off by other businesses that have closed down.

Candleworks was launched by making simple hand rolled beeswax candles. Beeswax is the ultimate natural recycled product. Beeswax is one of the most interesting natural substances used by human civilization. Beeswax has been in human use for over 50,000 years. Beeswax is produced by glands on the underside of the honeybee. The bee ingests plant sugars, and beeswax is a *biological waste product* produced along with honey. Honey bees use this wax to build their hives.

Beeswax collecting is a unique exercise in *interspecies material recycling*. Honey bees never re-use the wax that hives are constructed of. The bees build new hives from new wax deposits. Humans only collect beeswax *after* the honeybee has derived full use from it. Bee collectors gather in the used beeswax structures left behind in old hives as part of their honey harvest. The beeswax is then melted and filtered to clean out any foreign material. This process in no way harms the bee. In fact, beekeeping is a natural symbiotic relationship that is helpful to both humans and bees. Beekeepers provide shelter and nutrients to the bees. The bees, in trade, provide honey and beeswax for human use. This is nature's original "fair trade" system that serves as a model for our fair trade enterprise. At Candleworks, our workshop is an expanding beehive of creative activity.

Throughout history, beeswax has been a very valuable commodity. During feudal times, beeswax was the most valuable payment provided to the kingdom by the agrarian serfs. In modern times, beeswax is used for dental molds, as a key ingredient in natural cosmetics and for the making of the highest quality candles.

Beeswax is a wonderful material for candle making. It's own scent is distinctive and pleasant. We learned however, that the beeswax scent is strong enough that 100% beeswax should not be used to produce our aromatherapy candles. Candleworks created an innovative candle wax blend that includes a mix of vegetable wax and beeswax that carries aromatherapy scents very effectively. This wax blend led to our breakthrough phase of growth in the national candle industry.

Candleworks ships products to all 50 states and all 7 provinces in Canada in foam packing. We recycle this foam from a nearby giant aviation electronics plant, Rockwell International. Rockwell has thousands of electronic components shipped into their plant packed in fine foam and Styrofoam packing "peanuts". In the past, Rockwell International actually incurred significant additional manufacturing cost by paying to dump these packaging materials at the solid waste landfill. Candleworks ships fragile candles thousands of miles. We took these two problems, and through recycling Rockwell's packing materials, the two problems merged into one creative cost saving solution. Both companies now save time and money. Tons of waste no longer go to the local landfill.

The Lutheran Church calls us whenever they have old candle ends to throw away. The Catholic Church orders processional candles for their Easter Ceremonies. We make all of the new Catholic candles from recycled Lutheran candles. Through this *ecumenical recycling*, when both churches preach that there is "One True Light", they both now tell a proven truth!

At Candleworks, we even save waste wax scraped up from the workshop floor. We recycle it with sawdust from our wooden candle holder production. These two waste products combine to create a useful new product: fire-starter briquettes for fireplaces!

The only thing Candleworks does not recycle is money! Most small businesses just re-circulate and recycle existing cash in the local economy. Candleworks brings *new money* into our local economy. We export the goods we produce to all fifty states, all 7 provinces in Canada and to Europe, Australia and Asia. This creates new growth and jobs for our local economy.

Bootstrapper's Basic Skill #6: Discover the resources all around you. There are physical materials, creative ideas, time, labor and knowledge being wasted all around you. Re-capture this waste, recycle it into innovative, productive use.

Reader's notes:

How do I waste time, energy, money, and materials?

How can I recycle these wasted resources?

Chapter Seven
Profits through Principles;
The Corporation that Love Built

<u>Foundation principles of Candleworks:</u>

The most efficient and lasting way for society to create opportunity for disadvantaged persons, is to develop new employment opportunities. This way people claim their own self-worth. They create their own means to progress beyond their socio-economic disadvantage or disability. We involve people in creative interchange. We discover ability within disablity and find an advantage to overcome disadvantage.

AN ECONOMY OF FAIR GIVING AND RECEIVING IS THE FIRST FOUNDATION PRINCIPLE OF CANDLEWORKS.

Give a man a fish, he'll eat for a day.
Teach a man to fish, he'll eat for a lifetime.
      -TRADITIONAL CHINESE PROVERB

Our policy at Candleworks is that everyone deserves the *initial opportunity* for a job. Keeping the job is then the result of each person's own hard work. At Candleworks, management never "fires" anyone. However, workers can end their own job by not carrying out the responsibilities to Candleworks that they assume by accepting the job. We set very clearly stated work rules, defined quality standards and quotas for efficient, profitable productivity. If these expectations are not met by the worker, we have predetermined consequences that are communicated to all staff. A failure to carry out agreed on job responsibilities first brings the worker a verbal notice from their team leader. The next step in our process of established consequences is a written notice. If the employee still fails to take corrective action and meet their responsibilities, they're placed on a short suspension. The final step, if an employee does not choose to make progress, is termination of their job.

Candleworks has hired felons, known drug dealers and people with a laundry list of problems that would make most employers run the other way. We evaluate the *present*, not the past. Our employees include former heroin addicts and recovering alcolohics. A local upstanding citizen recently criticized us for assisting former criminals. If legitimate opportunities are not developed for a person who has had a criminal career, the only way we leave them to survive is through illegitimate means such as crime and drug dealing.

Most state governments spend more funds on prisons than on economic development. This is very short range thinking. This *vision deficit disorder* of our political leaders creates permanent problems instead of creating viable solutions. If the same funds were used to educate and create useful employment opportunities, our society could be transformed. Candleworks is building one small model of how an entire city, an entire state, an entire nation, a dynamic global economy *could work*. We *light one candle.*

In 1997, Candleworks was presented a Housing and Urban Development "Best Practice" award by President Clinton at the National Conference of Mayors. People are starting to notice the **Candleworks model.**

>Academics propose *theory*. Politicians set *policy*. Entrepreneurs shape *reality*.

*A university can spend $100,000 to *study* a problem.

*Governments spend $200,000 to *evaluate* a problem.

*A creative entrepreneur can make money and new jobs for others by *solving* the problem!

Candleworks is now providing effective international consulting on community problem solving and social entrepreneurship. Come and visit us, or Candleworks can send a dynamic training team to your community. <u>Contact us</u>: **Phone: 319**-354-7515 /**Fax**: 319-337-9034. You can find our **web page** at WWW.Candleworks.Org

While politicians engage in political debate about welfare reform, Candleworks engages in real world work place reform. We provide new opportunities for disenfranchised persons to provide their own welfare. Candleworks provides our workers an opportunity, not a free ride. Quality products are the only way we can keep our jobs secure for our entire work group. Creating quality products also generates self-esteem. This is not a charity. Candleworks competes without subsidy or special favor in the global marketplace. If a single person threatens our commitment to quality production and a happy, healthy workplace, they threaten everyone's job, not just their own. At Candleworks, all team leaders of our work groups have come to Candleworks with their own disadvantages or disabilities. We promote all team leaders *from the bottom up.* Our team leaders are fair, but demanding leaders. They've all been through a lifetime of bullshit, so they don't take any "bull" here. Team members pull their own weight, or they get a very clear message; *"We luv ya'...but, hasta la vista, baby- Come back when you grow up".*

Our doors often re-open for a returning "prodigal son" or two, who decide just that; Candleworks is a great place to grow up and get your life on track. Our written policies state that at Candleworks we accept that positive change can be brought about by anyone at anytime. Even a terminated employee can re-apply for a job six months after their dismissal.

Candleworks is definitely a corporation "that love built". This is *real love* however, not coddling or patronization. "Tough love" is a good definition. The love that is expressed by the Candleworks team is a love that expects and demands the best from one another. Enabling someone to continue with self destructive behavior of any kind is not real love.

The old model of the angry, tough boss that rules by intimidation is passé. *That method no longer works.* The old tough boss is really not tough at all. *He is a coward; a* coward that intimidates people and keeps them at a distance because he has a deep fear of human contact. A huge office desk, closed office doors and rule by a roar are all *barriers* that keep people at a safe distance from the fearful, cowardly boss.

CANDLEWORKS SECOND FOUNDATION PRINCIPLE IS THAT THE REAL MEASURE OF HUMAN PROGRESS IS THE QUALITY OF LIFE FOR THOSE ON THE *LOWEST* SOCIO-ECONOMIC TIER.

The history of social progress can be measured *economically:* entire nations, classes and races have gradually been included in the economic benefits of human society. This evolution reached its pinnacle in the United States in the twentieth century, and is now spreading globally in the information age. Observation of the natural environment demonstrates that life grows into more and more developed and organized states. *The opportunity for growth and activity is the primary need of all living organisms.*

Every individual is responsible for their own growth. The science of ecology demonstrates, however, that life only survives and grows *in community*. It's thus the responsibility of strong members of a community to assist disadvantaged persons to find opportunities to gain strength and grow. All then grow to a higher potential. We're *a unified life*, even if we don't realize that fact. By realizing it, we assist our own evolution.

THE THIRD FOUNDATION PRINCIPLE OF CANDLEWORKS IS *RECIPROCITY*: A BALANCED CYCLE OF INTERCHANGE.

The old model of charity, where there is an *imbalance* between the value transferred between the giver and receiver is a distortion of the nature of growth. The altruism of our new global culture must be "fair trade": Where a giver provides the receiver the opportunity to give in return *and in equal measure*. In this way the socially and economically disadvantaged climb up into an improved condition through reciprocal trade.

> *"Liberty requires the*
> *opportunity to make a living_*
> *a living which gives a man not*
> *only enough to live by,*
> *but something to live for."*
> -FRANKLIN D. ROOSEVELT

In the old model of charity, shelter, medical care, clothing or food were provided so that a disadvantaged person could *survive*. The only way a person can *thrive* is if they are provided an opportunity to contribute work and benefit to society. This way they also receive the "soul food" of community, self respect and purpose. The old welfare approach created a false system of "do-gooders" and "good for nothings". A do-gooder creates a self-serving sense of superiority, not a shared experience of opportunity and new growth.

In our dysfunctional social welfare system of giant government agencies and national charities, the *love* of real charity is replaced by cold bureaucratic processes. These systems devalue and disempower the recipients. The old welfare model leaves the middle class taxpayers feeling resentful and used. An antagonism of "us and them" is created between the middle class and the lower class, providing ease of control by the upper class. The human connection of real charity is non-existent in the depersonalized state welfare system. Meaningful acts of charity require *direct human contact* between the giver and receiver.

Opportunity for growth includes the inherent risk of failure. Life moves forward through risk taking. Candleworks' goal is to create an environment where progressive opportunities for growth match the participant's potential for growth. We start everyone at their own level. Since we work with people with a wide range of disabilities and abilities, we've created a work place with a *continuum of growth*. We don't expect that each employee will grow and produce at the same rate. We do expect that each person puts forth *100% effort.* Our workers evaluate one another.

Candleworks was set up as a relatively simple industry where people with very little work experience and physical limitations have the opportunity to start employment with simple tasks such as labeling and packaging and *work up* through the more challenging work of candle production and business management. This provides an opportunity for continuing growth.

OUR FOURTH FOUNDATION PRINCIPLE IS THAT EVERYONE NEEDS BASIC RESOURCES FOR A PURPOSEFUL LIFE:

1. the fulfillment of basic survival needs for food, shelter and safety (Candleworks provides direct housing and nutrition assistance for our staff through some very creative programs.)
2. the development of a sense of self worth and self-love is necessary for physical/mental health.
3. the ability to then express this self love as love and acceptance in community with others.
4. opportunities for learning, growth and self expression through a continuum of development.
5. the opportunity to be a self-sufficient social contributor that loves, works, gives and receives.

Self-sufficiency can only be achieved in a community of fair interchange. Humans are social by nature. Healthy humanhood is attained in community. Human isolation is a prime cause of physical and mental illness. Psychotics and sociopaths are the result of extreme human isolation; often originating with lack of human bonding in early childhood. Candleworks provides *remedial bonding* in a family-like work group. This method has proven effective for many staff who had maladjusted socially and had gone down the road of crime and substance abuse. Candleworks is a *safe place* where people turn themselves around and learn to love themselves, their work and one another.

Every thriving business is a highly organized community of dynamic growth and advancement. It's Candleworks goal to profit *through* our principles. The Latin root of profit is profectus. Profectus means *"to advance"*. In order for a business to sustain long term profit, the individuals in the business society must also be growing, advancing or "profiting". It is just as important for the business to also contribute to the advancement or *profit* of human society *as a whole.* Candleworks builds new community wealth. The traditional measure of profit, *surplus revenue* is a necessity for any business or other enterprise such as an educational or cultural institution to grow. With this holistic understanding of profit, the more profit that a company can generate, the more the company can contribute to the advancement of the company founders, the employees and society as a whole. Candleworks operates somewhat like an extended family in a traditional village. A traditional village provides communal love, safety and established structures of mutual responsibility. Growing up, we'd see the "Our Gang" Comedies; these "Little Rascals" were always cooking up a Depression Era scheme to make a buck or two to keep their club house going. "All for one and one for all" was the motto of the "Our Gang". "All for one and one for all" is the functional motto of Candleworks. We have a few rascals here also!

We take a liberal attitude toward personal and social needs and a conservative view toward creating a dynamic private business enterprise. This blend works. Candleworks operates with a "Republican" brain and a "Democratic" heart. Our balance is crucial.

Instead of just maximizing short term profits, wealth is shared at Candleworks. Scores of disadvantaged and disabled persons have been provided interest free loans to get out of depressing homeless shelters and into permanent homes so they can become stable employees. Through a joint effort with the City Housing Commission, Candleworks has assisted several of our employees to become permanent home owners. We're convinced that if *everyone* who is a part of Candleworks profits, our long term profits will be maximized. *We all work as a team with the same goals.*

Candleworks participates with a volunteer group in our community to operate "Table to Table", a food recovery program. We reclaim food destined for the dumpster from area grocery stores and bakeries. This food is then redistributed to Candleworks employees, and also to participants in twenty other community agencies that serve the needs of the poor, disabled, and socially disenfranchised. In it's first year, "Table to Table" has recovered and distributed 80 tons of food!

Candleworks crew members volunteer to distribute food through the "Table to Table" organization. Many of our staff had spent a portion of their lives hungry and homeless. Now they apply a very important life principle in their daily activity:

> *"To receive whatever you need most, first find a way to give it to others who need it more than you."*

Numerous hours of Candleworks' management time is spent each week assisting disabled staff to resolve medical needs. We assist people who'd been in trouble with the law to work through the legal system; so they can integrate back into the community as productive citizens. We work with former alcoholics and heroin addicts to overcome addictions to live productive lives again. Candleworks is actually a group of social misfits, who all somehow fit together. Together, we run a dynamic business enterprise that successfully competes in the global marketplace. People who'd been chronic tax burdens become hard-working tax-paying citizens. Life works at Candleworks, because love is the deep root of our work. Love is a practical principle. Candleworks supports our staff to grow and become strong, and thus we develop a strong, dynamic group.

THE FIFTH FOUNDATION PRINCIPLE OF CANDLEWORKS IS UNCONDITIONAL LOVE AND ACCEPTANCE:

How does this work? *Love* is a word not usually applied to the operation of a manufacturing plant, but *love* is the key ingredient of the success of Candleworks. *This is the Corporation that Love Built.* One very important aspect of real love is unconditional acceptance. Candleworks employs many people with a past of personal, social and legal problems. At Candleworks the past does not equal the future! We focus on the present. When a new employee walks through our door, <u>their past stays outside the door behind them</u>. We've never checked past references on any employee. Our staff are only judged on their commitment and performance *in the present*. Our only application papers are a set of federal and state tax forms and an agreement to work for the first thirty days to prove ability and commitment during a probationary training period. *A new life starts as you walk in the Candleworks door.*

The founders of Candleworks worked the first three years without regular pay. At the same time we paid our staff regular paychecks and lent out the profit of the company to get our work force out of jails and shelters. This is not charity; permanent homes help our team become permanent Candleworks staff. This is a win/win effort with mutual benefits. We drove to our first key marketing meetings in run down old cars. Our first imports into Canadian retail chains were delivered in a rusty twenty year old cargo van. During lean times, we'd literally empty our pockets of our last quarters and dimes so that staff would have a meal or bus fare home. We founded Candleworks when I was unemployed. Our family lived in an abandoned tenement building, hanging on the brink of street level homelessness. Candleworks was created as a way to give away what our family needed the most. Now we also get what we need. Our business is based on the perennial wisdom of life, not just business strategy.

Whatever you most need in life, the best way to get it is to help someone else get it who needs it more than you.
  -JOE TYE, AUTHOR, *NEVER FEAR, NEVER QUIT* (Rafe's Law)

All Candleworkers work very hard for Candleworks because the founders of Candleworks work very hard for them. We all work in a system of fair interchange. Many manufacturing companies are set up by wealthy investors. Candleworks was set up by founders and workers in an *equal state of poverty and economic challenge*. At the time the Richards family started Candleworks, I'd just been laid off from work. We were living under the official federal poverty income level in an abandoned New York City tenement building. We needed work and a home, so we found those who needed these things more than we did. We found a way to give what we also needed to receive. Love works.

Because of our bootstrapping origins, Candleworks has evolved with an open, egalitarian, participatory management structure. We're all in this together. Candleworks is an activity of *real compassion:* the old welfare model is a pitiful example of *false compassion: pity*. State welfare is a paternalistic process created by an upper class that throws a bone or two to the underclass that they pity. Since the costs of welfare

are mainly borne by the middle class, this is a very unfair structure. Real compassion empowers the recipient. False compassion (pity) disempowers the recipient. Compassion is a powerful healing force.

Real compassion is a human emotion that can only be experienced *by equals*. Human compassion knows no difference in station or class, just a *mutual recognition of the challenges of life*. We can work through these challenges much more productively if we can "feel together". Com-passion is defined literally as *feeling in unity*. Compassion is simply the bond of human love. Once in a while a team leader at Candleworks slips backward. People they once helped up, now turn back around and return the hand up. We each give one another a continuing hand up in an endless chain of human compassion and mutual understanding. At Candleworks, *"we light up the world one life at a time."* As a group this light is multiplied. This is a bright place indeed. People love to visit Candleworks. Light, love and joy are tangible qualities here.

One of the most important principles of Candleworks and life is *"the more you can laugh, the more you can love"*. Laughter opens the heart and the lungs for full life experience. The root word of humor is "umor" which literally means *fluid*. Humor releases friction and anger. Humor is the grease that keeps the wheels of life turning. Humor fills the days at Candleworks and keeps us all laughing, loving and working. We laugh even when difficult times come. We take our work seriously, and ourselves lightly. To prepare to write this book, I asked each of our Candlemakers to list the *funniest* thing that has ever happened at Candleworks. <u>Here's a sample of their replies:</u>

- *"Feeling a little woozy and wobbly from all the heady candle scents in the air."* -**Lynn**

-"We all laughed when "Puppers"(our four legged Candleworker) got picked up three days in a row and sent to doggy jail. We all had to chip in to post his bail, 'cause it went up $5 more dollars each day." **-Pat**

-"It does take a "rocket scientist" to make candles right. There's more to candles than meets the eye." **-Mike**

"I thought I was in a new T.V. situation comedy when we were just two hundred candles away from shipping out a $50,000 order, when we ran out of our last penny of operating cash. To get final $5 bucks we needed for set screws to tighten wick in the molds, we all searched the curbs for pop cans. With everyone helping, in a few minutes we had enough cans to make it happen. We took the cans to the grocery store, got our $5 can refund and went across the street to the hardware store to buy the set screws! We got the shipment out! In about 6 weeks the customer paid us the 50 grand so we could keep Candleworks movin' along!" **-Dana**

-"I laughed and laughed when we first started making our "vegetarian candles" for the natural products market. The first truck load of vegetable-base wax arrived from down south in Memphis, Tennessee, marked in big letters **KOSHER**. We concocted an imaginary bearded fellow we call **"Rabbi Billy-Bob Ruben"** blessing all the vegetable wax shipped to Candleworks from down south in Dixie! "**-Art**

-"We hit the nail on the head when we realized that C.E.O. on our company founder's letterhead stood for "**C**razy **E**nough to **O**wn it!" -**Jane**

Love is the primary currency of life. Giving and receiving love is the actual economy of life. In the final analysis, we are all in this life with <u>one purpose</u>: to learn how to give and receive love in abundance.

Love is the actual motivator of our labor. Most professionals, laborers, and bootstrap entrepreneurs work very hard because they want a better home or improved life for their spouse, a loved one or their children. A few misguided people work for the love of money or power, but this is actually a small minority.

Bootstrapper's Basic Skill #7: Base your work on love; love of self and family, love of your work, love of your co-workers and love of the customers you serve. Love connects us with a deep source of life and energy. Live, laugh, work and love in abundance.

> *Work is love made visible."*
> -KAHLIL GIBRAN, *The Prophet*

Reader's notes:

What work do you love to do?

How do you think you could earn a living by doing this work that you love?

How can you learn to love the job where you currently work?

What act of creative "intrapraneurship" can you carry out to transform your present place of employment?

Chapter Eight
Each Worker has a Story
Assessing Our Assets

At **Candleworks** our most important assets are all of the **Candleworkers.** Our original group of workers were living homeless on the streets of New York. H.U.D. statistics indicate that the average American family hangs on the brink; just two pay checks away from homelessness. Any health or employment crisis can place a person over the edge and into the street. Candleworks was created as a means to develop employment for people who for one reason or another had been left out of the job market.

In Iowa, 60% of all disabled persons are unemployed. In the whole country, 75% are left out of the job market. Diversity is discussed but rarely acted on. Diversity at Candleworks is a reality, not a buzzword.

Candleworks was bootstrapped up from nothing. We had no assets other than diverse people who really wanted to work to better their lives. Our first candles were rolled *by hand* by people who lived homeless on the streets of New York City. We had no equipment, we had no money. Our only tools were the hands of each person, and the desire in each person's heart. Our raw materials were wax, sweat, joy and love.

The story of Candleworks is the story of our people:

Hilda's Story

Hilda had been an independent fashion designer. She made stage costumes and street fashion for some of the luminaries of New York's music club scene. During the heady 80's and 90's Hilda was drawn into the cocaine euphoria of the New York night life of her fashion clientele. After a year or two, her ticket for entry into that glitzy world, her skills to create fine fashion, fell by the wayside. Hilda began a rapid downslide. Cocaine and other drugs were no longer just an accessory to this high fashion life, they had become her sole obsession. Hilda lost it all; her family, her career, her dignity. Soon, there was no longer any money for the high priced designer drugs. Cheap wine would do. She slid down to the gutter, to the life of a street alcoholic.

After two degrading years, invisible on the streets of New York, Hilda finally found her way into the shelter for women operated by Sister Marian on New York's Lower East Side. Hilda struggled to pull her life back together. She reclaimed her self respect. She started making hundreds and hundreds of candles. Hilda was the most productive candle maker in the early development phase of Candleworks. Her quantity and quality were unmatched. Hilda saved as much money as she could from her candlemaking enterprise to buy fine cloth in New York's fashion district. She rediscovered her design and seamstress skills. She started up her own small business making fine silk scarves for fashion boutiques in Manhattan.

Jafar's Story

Jafar immigrated to New York City from Western Africa. In Harlem, he met and married an American wife. They quickly had two sons, just 9 months apart. Jafar had been working double shifts driving a Gypsy cab (an unlicensed taxi) so that he could save up money to become a licensed owner/operator of a New York taxi. One night, Jafar came home to their tiny Harlem apartment to find his two infant sons crying, hungry and wet. The money he'd saved to buy a legal taxi was missing; gone with his wife to support the drug habit that had taken her into the streets of Harlem. The addictions of Jafar's wife exploded his American Dream.

Without cash for the monthly rent, Jafar's landlord tossed him and his little children into the cold streets of New York in the middle of the night, in the middle of winter. Jafar's run down gypsy cab finally gasped to a smoky final halt in a back alley of Harlem. They lived in this abandoned car until a New York health agency found them living in these desperate conditions. As a homeless single father, he was referred to a shelter for homeless families. Candleworks set Jafar up as an independent home-based worker. He enthusiastically took up the candle making trade. This allowed him to earn a living at home, and care for his infant sons.

John K's Story

John K. was living the dream life of a 1970's small town teenager. *American Grafitti*, manifest. He had his own car. He was an Iowa State Champ on the High School Wrestling team. Girls paid him lots of attention. One night, a drunken drive down the highway to party with friends turned his dream into a nightmare.

His once agile body was as twisted and wrecked as his once shiny car. His quick thinking brain was slowed to a struggling crawl by a serious brain injury. The slurred speech of youthful drunkenness now became a permanent life long disability.

At the same time Candleworks set up shop in Iowa, John had come in from the storm of several years as a homeless street alcoholic to take a shower and clean up his life at the Emergency Housing Shelter in Iowa City. John only had use of one hand. The beeswax sheets that we made into candles were 16 inches long; too long to manage a straight roll with one hand. John created his own new way to make the candles. He cut the wax in half to a manageable 8 inches, so each beeswax sheet made one perfectly matched pair. These pairs sold the best of all. Soon all the candlemakers switched over to make their candles John's way. John's pride in creating his own candlemaking method instilled the sense of self-worth and esteem he had not felt since he won medals for his high school team more than twenty years ago. John was shining. *He had discovered his ability within his disability.*

When John first struggled down the steps to our workshop, his body and clothes literally wreaked of the life of a homeless street alcoholic. With his new found self esteem, he set out to clean up his whole life. He started laundering his clothing, and used the shower in the Candleworks shop. It's nearly impossible for a homeless person to get a job and a home when they no longer have access to the basics of life that we take for granted: a regular shower, a place to be well rested for work, a phone to set up job interviews. At Candleworks, we provide these basic necessities along with a job to bootstrap back to full participation in the human community.

John became a candle rolling demon. In just a few weeks, he'd saved up enough cash from his work to get on our phone and call about small apartments listed in the local newspaper. Through his own effort, he lined up a lease with an apartment developer's wife. He moved in the same night. A few months later, the husband attempted to evict John, even though he had religiously paid his rent exactly on time every month.

The only reason the landlord gave was that John walked and talked strange. The landlord said that John was different, so he made people uncomfortable. Candleworks assisted John with filing a housing discrimination complaint with the local Human Rights Commission. This discrimination case was also filed with the federal agency authorities at H.U.D. (Housing and Urban Development). Candleworks staff helped John fight his housing discrimination case all the way to the Iowa Supreme Court. John won a cash settlement, his dignity and his legal right to a permanent residence.

Dana's Story

Dana had a close family, growing up with several brothers in a small town in Central Iowa. On a weekend hunting trip with his brothers, Dana was injured by an accidental gun discharge. The bullet ripped through his spinal cord, leaving Dana paraplegic at the age of 15. Dana had been in and out of hospitals and rehabilitation centers for most of his life, for serious health problems, his disability and chronic abuse of a plethora of dangerous drugs.

Dana was living homeless in a run-down van, outfitted with a wheelchair lift and hand brakes. He'd heard about Candleworks from other people living on the street and under bridges in the Iowa City area. Dana came rolling into Candleworks at the time we were still working in a makeshift workshop in an abandoned building. We'd just been selected to launch a new line of hand poured pillar candles for a major national chain of stores. Dana quickly became an expert at deftly re-stringing the candle molds. His accident had left him with just the use of his arms and hands, his legs were rendered useless. Now Dana had a way to use the strength and dexterity of his hands in a very creative way. Candleworks fosters *adaptability.*

For the first few months of work, Dana still lived in his van. The police stopped him for driving with a suspended license. They impounded his van. I went into the Judge's Chamber to protest. I reasoned with the Judge that with Dana, his van was a matter of life and security. His van was not just for joy-riding. This was like taking the shell from a tortoise. This van was both Dana's mobility *and his hom*e. Reason and Law are often two different things. Dana lost his mobility and shelter. The Judge just seemed numb and bored.

Soon Dana earned enough money to rent his own apartment to end years of living homeless, drunk, drugged and depressed. A local real estate developer advertised a one bedroom *"handicapped accessible"* apartment. Dana didn't want to pass up his opportunity to finally have a home of his own. He rushed over to the office. He paid the rent on the spot. He set out to move in. When he arrived, Dana discovered that this *"handicapped accessible"* apartment had a bathroom door too narrow for him to wheel into and a mailbox much too high for him to reach from his wheelchair.

Dana's courteous calls to his landlord to correct these access problems went unheeded. From our experience with John K's case, we were familiar with how to file formal housing discrimination complaints. We helped Dana file initial papers with the City Human Rights Commission. Within a few days after delivery of legal papers to the landlord's office, the corrective access construction was complete. Dana now had what he needed; a home and self-respect. He voluntarily dropped the housing discrimination complaint.

Candleworks advocacy for homeless, disadvantaged and disabled persons in regard to employment, housing, health, nutrition, and legal issues was noticed by many leaders in our community. In 1994, Candleworks was thus named "Business of the Year" by the Human Rights Commission. John K., now sober, well-groomed and in fresh clothes proudly accompanied the Candleworks founders to accept this community recognition. Several community leaders who had personally turned John K. in for public intoxication in the past came forward to congratulate him on the community award and his personal transformation.

The following year, Candleworks nominated **World Marketplace**, a local retail store, for the Human Rights Commission's "Business of the Year" award. This was in recognition of their efforts to market products made by local self-help economic development projects like Candleworks and from village craft co-ops all over the world. Dana joined in with the ceremony and conversed with members of City Council. Dana's Judge was there.

Dana has now progressed even further. He *owns* his home, and operates his own home-based specialty candle making business part-time, while he continues to work for Candleworks. Dana is a daily bootstrapper; on many days when a ride was not available to get to work, he set out rolling himself the five miles to Candleworks in his wheelchair. How many of us have that kind of motivation to get to work?

Casper's Story

At age 49, Casper lost the factory job he'd had for many years. Jobless, he sunk into a pit of drinking, endless T.V. sitcoms and despair. After months of trying to keep the family together on one factory paycheck, Casper's tired and troubled wife gave him an angry ultimatum: "turn off the damn T.V. and get a job, or get out!" Casper got out. He drank more and more. He was found drunk, cold and near death, in a gutter right at the curb of a local hospital. A passerby hauled him into the emergency room. Casper was nursed back to life and referred down the block to the homeless shelter.

Casper had worked as a shipping clerk at the factory, so we set him up as the shipping manager for Candleworks. He took to this job like a duck to water. He'd show up at work earlier and earlier, just so he could see what orders customers from distant destinations had faxed into our office overnight. When his arrival time came earlier than my wake up time, I just gave him a key.

Casper loved imagining the far off cities he was shipping candles to. One day, we had large shipments going to Chicago and then to Canada. Casper and I jumped into a rusty old van with 180,000 miles on the speedometer and half as many on the tires. We drove our products direct to the customer. Casper was a country boy who'd never been to the big city. His eyes lit up with the shimmering skyline as we scooped the loop of Chicago's "Gold Coast". We meandered along the late night magic of Lakeshore Drive.

We delivered our goods to a group of up-scale stores on Michigan Avenue and Clark St. Casper got to see with his eyes the destinations of the candle shipments that he had only imagined before. This called for celebration. We took the elevator to the very top of the towering John Hancock Building in the heart of downtown Chicago. We sat down at the polished bar in the exclusive cafe at the top of the skyscraper. The classy waitress looked inquisitively at Casper and I in our flannel workshirts and wax spotted jeans among all the Armani and Brook's Brothers clad clientele. I ordered a $7 beer, Casper happily ordered a $5 coke.

On the spot, Casper quit drinking on his own, no forced de-tox, no treatment program. He did it because he needed to quit, and he wanted to quit. The despair and desperation that led him into deep alcoholism were no longer present. *The only real cure is to get rid of the cause.* Casper had accomplished his cure for himself at Candleworks. That $5 coke was worth every penny. Casper savored every sip as he gazed out into the amazing lights of Chicago. At 100 stories high, Casper was on top of the world.

That one coke and a beer took a sizable bite out of our travel budget! We only had enough cash for gas and a sack of groceries to get us on to our delivery in Canada. We drove all night long. Casper and I never slept that night. As we crossed over the high arch of the Ambassador Bridge into Canada, the dawn light lit up Casper's eyes like a new born babe.

Harry and Sally

When Harry Met Sally, *Candleworks style...* Harry lived on the street. He survived by picking up soda cans, dumpster diving and petty thievery. Sally was disabled and lived in a sheltered community group home. Their paths crossed when they both came to work at Candleworks. Love blossomed. A wedding date was set. For their honeymoon trip, they made the next Candleworks delivery to our customers in Canada.

Harry and Sally worked on candles as a team. They saved their money, and planned to have a family. Together, they had enough income to rent a beautiful home on the banks of the river. Harry and Sally held hands as they told their Candleworks story to a Chicago television crew. They now had income, a home, self respect and set out to build a new life together. Life at Candleworks went well for Harry and Sally for a couple of years. Harry was staying out of trouble with the law. Then, one day the cops showed up. Harry had slipped back into his old ways of taking what he needed rather than earning it. Sally kept her chin up, and kept on working. She now has a new partner and her progress continues.

Candleworks has a long list of success stories, but we don't bat 1000 every season. Candleworks has proven to be a catalyst for change in many peoples lives. The bottom line, however, is that this success is up to each person individually. *We can lead a horse to water, but we can't make them drink.*

Larry's Story

At the homeless shelter Casper had shared a bunk bed with Larry. Larry was now 62. He had spent his life as a proud carpenter and craftsman. For twenty years he had operated his own independent building and contracting business; building in Iowa during the warm months of the Spring, Summer and Fall, and migrating each Winter to Arizona to sell his trade in the warm sunny Southwest. He and his wife were not rich, but they prospered with the basics of the American Dream: a home in Iowa, another in Arizona and a nice camper truck to transport them back and forth as the seasons changed. Life was good. They had left one item out of their self-employment financial plan; *a health insurance policy.* Cancer struck Larry's wife like a bolt of Iowa summer lightning. She deteriorated quickly and died in pain. Larry drank. Larry found it difficult to work. The hospital costs took it all. Larry lost everything.

From a life of financial independence, Larry found himself in the homeless shelter. Candleworks had just found an abandoned building by the River on the same day that the landlord showed up with his bulldozer to tear it down. It had been flooded out and left after the Great Floods of the Spring of '93. We made a deal with the landlord that if we cleaned it up, he'd let us rent it for the value the lot had as a mobile home site: $150 per month. He parked the 'dozer and we got to work.

Our new makeshift workshop building needed a carpenter's care and an electrician's expertise. Larry needed a reason to live and a job. He set out to single-handedly reclaim our abandoned building. He wired us up to electrical service, he put glass in the windows and locks on the doors. Candleworks now had a workshop. Larry had a job as our resident handyman and troubleshooter. He built innovative candlemaking tools and equipment. He rebuilt his life. Unfortunately, cancer got him too, just three years after it took away his wife. Larry had found his life again at Candleworks though, just before he died. Death is a reality that we all face. Larry found the strength to face it with dignity rather than in despair.

Mick's Story

Mick wandered into Candleworks just after his trip around the world with the more famous Mick of Rolling Stones fame. Our candlemaking Mick had been traveling all over the world with a long list of famous people in his private helicopter. These were wondrous trips, *but they all took place in Mick's mind.* The volunteer shrink that visited the homeless shelter called his adventures *schizophrenia*. Mick didn't mind the label. He enjoyed his life *with* all the trips.

He told all the Candlemakers that he'd come to invest a million dollars in Candleworks to make our business grow just like his last entrepreneurial venture: *Texas Instruments*. Harold, one of our other Candlemakers asked Mick if he could buy stock in Candleworks. Mick said sure. Harold said he wanted to buy 51% of all Candleworks stock. Mick got a shy smile on his face and said: "No way man... then you'd fire me!"

Mick worked diligently at Candleworks for more than 6 months. He earned his way out of the homeless shelter and into a private apartment. One day he left word with a friend at Candleworks that he was heading off to Texas again. He must have gotten word that Texas Instruments needed his executive expertise more than Candleworks did. Mick said he was now their new C.E.O.

At Candleworks we accept people just as they are. Our entire team do our best to foster life improvement and support positive change, but each person makes their own choices. Mick chose to head on down the road.

Steve and Mark, A Father and Son Story

Steve had been a concert conductor and his son Mark was trained as an opera singer. As Steve entered his elderly years, the classical music world doors closed on him. Father and son taught music lessons in whatever music store would hire them. They then put their piano and voice skills together and set out on the road as a lounge act. Money and fortune faded. On one of their coast to coast treks, they ran out of cash and prospects right in the middle of the country: Iowa. From the concert stage to an Iowa City homeless shelter, their life had all the ups and downs of a game of musical chairs. They spoke of Royal relatives in Europe, but they were now broke and on the road.

On their very first day of work, I found Steve and Mark sauntering in the rain back to the bus stop. I asked them what they were looking for. They said they thought they had the address of a place recommended for employment, but when they opened the door they were greeted by "unsavory characters". I laughed and brought them back in to our candle workshop. Steve and Mark put down their umbrellas, took off their matching tweed coats, and shook the rain off their finely pressed clothes. They took their seats at the candle packaging table in between two ex-convicts and went to work. In the corporate world, diversity is a hot buzzword, at Candleworks diversity of another dimension is our daily reality: people of all ages, all backgrounds, many races, languages, nationalities, the able bodied and disabled all work together. From his first hesitant days mixing in with our motley crew, the finely coifed, well mannered and elderly Steve eventually joined in enthusiastically. He offered his fatherly advice to ex-drunks, ex cons and street people. One day, Steve turned to me and said of Candleworks: *"I guess we're all just a group of misfits here... that all fit together."* Nothing could describe the place better.

The next week our quality work teams orchestrated a great "pot-luck" Thanksgiving feast. Steve played the piano and sang, leading the whole candleworking crew in a sing-a-long of old standards. A few days later, Steve died of a heart attack. His son, Mark stayed on working with Candleworks. We had become his new family.

Jane's Story

Steve and Mark had been introduced to us by Jane. They had all met at a transitional living facility after leaving the homeless shelter. After college, Jane had set out on her own to live an independent life far from the Iowa farm family where she had grown up. She worked on the East Coast. She worked on the West Coast. She was thousands of miles from her home, but the emotional history of her family traveled with her. Thousands of miles could not separate her from her past. Outwardly, her family were proud, healthy Iowa farmers. Privately, dysfuntional patterns tore away at the family's roots.

The emotional weight of her own unresolved family relationships and her own internal struggle to claim her identity as an adult closed in on Jane. She developed panic disorder and agoraphobia. She became housebound. Her panic and fear kept her from going out and getting employment. Jane ended up jobless, penniless, and eventually homeless. Her panic disorder left Jane disabled and living on Social Security.

Candleworks accepts people just as they are, and provides a place for them to gain strength and put their life back in order at their own pace. At first, Jane worked at home where she felt safe from the panic and fear. Gradually, Jane discovered that since her fear was within, she must conquer it there, *inside*. Realizing that the fear did not originate outside of her door, she came out more and more, working up to full time work right in the Candleworks manufacturing plant. Jane gained strength, overcame her fear and voluntarily contacted Social Security to end her disability benefits. Jane became a team leader, and she now participates in the management of Candleworks. Jane now provides counsel and intervention to assist other staff work through their own emotional challenges. She now gives away what she's received.

Mike's Story

Mike had grown up in an Iowa youth shelter. He married young. He had kids and grandkids before he was very old himself. At some point the pressures of life weighed heavy on the marriage. Mike left Iowa and headed for the West Coast. He drifted into the San Francisco fog of weed and the world of the Grateful Dead. When he had employment, Mike spent time caring for the elderly and the dying as a home health care and hospice worker. This was a caring job, yet with a high emotional toll. Sometimes Mike sought shelter from the pain of this work in alcohol. Alcohol use became alcoholism. Sometimes for months at a time Mike lived on the street, and slept in Golden Gate Park.

One of the most important connections Mike has in life are his daughters. He cares a lot about them. They care deeply about him. They'd been out of touch for years. They sensed their father was having difficulty out in California. Mike's daughters, Tina and Tammy, called the San Francisco police to track him down as a missing person. As an amazing coincidence, Mike had been hauled in on a false arrest that week and released. Because of their error, the police had the information to connect Mike and his daughters. Tammy and Tina sent their dad a bus ticket. Jerry Garcia of the Grateful Dead died. The ticket was to leave two days before the Grand Memorial to Jerry in San Francisco. Mike missed the bus and went to one last celebration of the life of the Dead.

Tammy and Tina worried about their dad. Mike showed up late, but happy to be back near his family. Mike decided to stay on in Iowa to be near those that he loves. Penniless, homeless and a bit hung over from a recent drunk, Mike found his way into Candleworks. He's now become a team leader and is working hard to put his life on track for himself and his loved ones.

Fred's Story

Fred is a hard workin' man. Fred also is a hard drinkin' man. Sometimes after working long days as a carpenter, long distance truck driver and other honest hard labor, Fred felt like having a beer. Eventually, it came to a point where Fred was no longer having the beer; *the beer was having Fred.*

Rather than feeling like he wanted a drink, Fred got to the point where he really needed a drink. More and more alcohol led to deeper and deeper problems with the law. One drunken driving charge and your in trouble. Two drunken driving charges and your up a deep river with a broken paddle. In Iowa, after three drunken driving charges the judge can declare your offense a felony, and toss you in prison. Fred's #3 had him hanging at the brink.

Fred had started working at Candleworks just before he was called before the bench. Fred's court appointed attorney called Candleworks. I went to court with Fred and told the judge about the responsibilities that Fred had taken on as the new shipping manager for Candleworks. The judge saw that this man could turn things around and gave him *one last chance.* Fred finally works himself off of probation this next month. He'll finally be free of the legal system after a long, long time of being down by law.

José and Luis, American Dream El Norté

One day I dropped in at the homeless shelter to tell the director that we needed more help to get a large candle order produced and shipped out. She sent me a father and son team, José and Luis. José had worked as a legal alien with a green card as an agricultural worker for many years. During one of José 's trips into Texas for employment, 16 years ago, Luis was born in Houston. Luis had grown up in Mexico. Luis was legally an American Citizen. José and Luis had just made a north bound trek by hitchhiking and bus to Iowa. Here, Luis could claim his birthright as an American citizen. In Iowa, Luis has the benefit of an education in America. Luis works at Candleworks part time and goes to High School full time. He's learning English quickly and gets good grades. José supports himself and Luis and all the family back in Mexico by working at Candleworks and moonlighting at another factory job just across the railroad tracks from our plant.

Al's Story

Al had grown up as a big, strong strapping farm kid. In the past, kids like Al eventually took over the family farm. Al's life path had a radical detour with severe health problems. He ended up in Iowa City, disabled and without employment. He was referred to Candleworks by Goodwill Industries.

On a farm, if it breaks you fix it. Self-sufficiency comes second nature to kids growing up on a farm. Al took this native skill many steps further by taking mechanical training at a local community college. Al has now found his place as the equipment and mechanical maintenance manager for Candleworks. Al also whips up a great potato salad and heavenly deviled eggs. He takes charge of our employee potluck lunch every Friday.

Elton's Story

Elton had rambled about the United States for most of his adult life, not quite finding his place in the world. He filled the empty feelings inside of himself with enough alcohol to fell a horse. A kind elderly man in Nebraska offered Elton a place to come in from life's cold. The two of them operated a simple bicycle repair shop. Elton finally felt like he had found a home. The kind man died unexpectedly, leaving Elton homeless and untethered. Elton headed East with a bike he loved and a load of bicycle parts tossed in the back of a rusted out car with more miles on it than a car should ever have. Halfway across Iowa, on Interstate 80, the rusted out muffler fell off. A Highway Patrolman stopped Elton, and impounded his car in a tiny one horse town. Elton was stranded, knowing no one, no cash, no home, no direction. He got the bicycle he loved out of the dead hulk of a car, loaded his few possessions into a back pack and started pedaling toward the sunset. In the dark he found his way to the homeless shelter. In the morning he found his way to Candleworks.

Elton arrived on the scene at Candleworks just as we acquired our first piece of industrial scale candle production machinery; an electronic filler conveyor line. This machine increased our production capability by 500%. During the first month of operation, we produced an order of 80,000 holiday candles for Biolage/Matrix (a division of Bristol Meyer Squibb).

From Elton's years as a bicycle mechanic, he gained a good grasp of the workings of machinery. Elton became the filler machine operator. He developed a love/hate relationship with this machine. It provided him with a job and new purpose in life, but working out the bugs in the new machine caused him great frustration. This frustration led to several relapses into serious problem drinking. Over the last few months Elton has gained control over both the machine and his own drinking problem. He has found a new home and a new sense of balance. Life is not easy, but life is now working for him. At Candleworks, Elton has found a place in life.

Manfredo and Lesbia's Love Story

Manfredo and Lesbia fell in love while growing up in Guatemala. Manfredo's father became entangled in the persistent political conflicts of his homeland. Like so many other villagers, he "disappeared". Manfredo sensed that his own safety was now compromised. Manfredo escaped through the dense rain forest and steep mountains of Northern Guatemala. He traveled through the dense jungle under cover of deep night, illuminating his path with a torch. After a long struggle in Mexico, Manfredo made it to California. He found work, enrolled in college, and sent for Lesbia. Manfredo and Lesbia are now the proud parents of three daughters. They both hold team leader positions with Candleworks and are saving to buy a home.

Candleworks has become very multi-lingual. We have workers from several nations. Manfredo has a good command of both English and Spanish, so he provides the bridge of understanding with our Hispanic staff. This year, Candleworks is expanding our work with a sister candle plant that will be operated by disabled people in Spain. We're taking our message of *"finding the ability within disability"* global. The world is now our village. Our connection in Spain originally developed through communications over the World Wide Web. Manfredo will serve as our visiting technical consultant in Spain. Candleworks provides consulting services in many parts of the world to create economic self-sufficiency for disabled and disadvantaged persons. We do this through our training and consulting organization: **I-can**. (International Creative Ability Network). If your community needs assistance, call I-Can at 319-354-7515 The I-Can brochure is printed at the back of this book.

Susan's Story

Susan had held a professional job. Unexpectedly, Susan had a stroke when she was twenty-eight, just as her career was getting into gear. Susan's former employers saw her differently, now disabled. When she came to Candleworks, we looked for the ability beyond that disability. Susan has full use of her arm and hand on one side. Her other side has limited motion due to the stroke. Susan has learned to be a candlemaker, filling molds with one hand. Susan may just have full use of just one hand, but she has double the motivation of most people. Even our candlemakers with full use of two hands fill molds with a pitcher of wax in *one hand.* Susan is very flexible at work. She jumps right in and efficiently carries out whatever tasks are necessary to keep the candles moving. Susan laughs at everyone's jokes. She keeps the morale of the candle crew high.

Beth's Story

Beth was a championship athlete in High School. She went to a small university in Iowa with a scholarship in 3 collegiate sports. Beth was studying to share this athletic ability with young people as a Physical Education teacher. In the prime of her life, at the edge of her life's dream, Beth was struck with Multiple Sclerosis. Beth's life had been built around her physical abilities. Now she faced the serious debilitating effects of M.S. Beth came to Candleworks to find a productive new way to live her life. At Candleworks Beth is a role model of meeting adversity with a cheerful, strong attitude. This cheer comes through very strong in Beth's voice, so she is now training as our customer service phone manager. At Candleworks our goal is to find the ability within each disability. Beth carries out marketing and service calls to our customers in all 50 states. At Candleworks, our motto is: *"We light up the world, one life at a time".* Beth lights up Candleworks one day at a time.

Pat's Story

Pat's whole life was dedicated to her children, her husband and home. Family was the focus of her life. Pat had artistic ability and studied Art in College, but she set her personal interests aside to give 100% to her family life. Pat's home was her life and her world. Pat's husband's interest wandered from the central concern of home. He left home to go off with his secretary. Pat's home crumbled. Pat's world fell apart.

At age 50, a displaced homemaker has a very difficult time finding a new place in the world. Pat lived homeless and aimless for several years. She lived out of her car and crowded into a spare room of relatives if the winter got too cold.

Pat came to Candleworks more than a year ago and has been quickly transforming her life. She now holds the respect of herself and her co-workers as a team leader. She oversees the final finishing and packaging of hundreds of thousands of candles each year. Pat's the Queen of Productivity. Pat is no longer homeless. Through her income with Candleworks she has now become a homeowner. Her home is now a comfortable safe place to share with her children and grandkids.

Art's Story

Art had it all; a professional career and a wife with her own profession. Together they had two beautiful children and owned a home on a pleasant shady street. Drinking went from a way to relax after work to a way of living. Alcohol took over and stole the dream away. Art had it all, then Art lost it all. Divorce. Depression. Art's children moved away when their mother had a professional opportunity in a far away town. Insult added to injury, and at first more drinking covered the pain. After Art lost his family, Art lost his purpose. Then Art lost his home. From an ideal middle class life to homelessness is a steep drop. Art fell all the way.

When Art was at his weakest point in life, he found strength deep inside of himself. Art found the *courage* to face the alcohol square in the face. He sought help with treatment. Art won the battle. Candleworks offered him a new lease on life. Art brings to us his 20 years of expertise in the candlemaking trade. Art's family had operated a candle factory for years. Art needed us and we needed him; Divine order.

Art has now had his drinking under control for more than a year. One day, Art just ordered in pizza for the entire candle crew. As everyone happily munched down, we realized it was Art's anniversary; one year of his new productive life at Candleworks.

At Candleworks, the operating principle is this: *"If you really need something, find someone who needs it more than you do, and give it to them."* Art is practicing this; he now leads a self-help group at Candleworks to help other employees who have not yet won their battle with addiction.

One of the happiest days ever at Candleworks, was when all of the Candleworks clan, joined in with Art's reunion with his kids. Now in their teens, they came to see Art's taper and pillar candle operation and spend all day with their Dad.

Amparo and Olga's Family Ties

Amparo led the way from her home in Michoacan, a rural region in the southern area of Mexico to find a better life in the United States. Many families in Mexico live with a severe shortage of financial opportunity. They compensate for this lack of money by building large extended families that work together to provide life's necessities. It takes strength, faith and courage to seek out your place in a new country where custom and language are unfamiliar. The United States was built by the strength and courage of immigrants from all over the world. New immigrants keep this strength and courage alive and growing. This is why the U.S. leads the global economy.

Amparo first found restaurant work in West Virginia. Her search for a permanent job and home led her to North Carolina, California, and then to Iowa. Once

Amparo was established with a secure home and a job, she helped her niece, Olga also move to the United States. Olga first found Candleworks, and then brought her Aunt Amparo to work with us too. Family ties are deep and strong in the Hispanic culture. At Candleworks, we are building an extended family that embraces all cultures. Diversity is our strength.

Bob's Story

Bob is a little past 50. He had a good job as a truck driver. On a day off, Bob was riding a bicycle down a steep hill. He hit a bump and went head over heels. The bike crashed to a halt, and Bob kept rolling on down the hill. When he woke up in the hospital, his eyesight and memory were no longer complete. He'd tumbled down a hill, so now society labeled him *over the hill.* For six years Bob could not find a new job. After a productive life, this left him feeling without purpose. Goodwill Industries then finally referred Bob to Candleworks. Bob loves his job. He tells us how much he loves it just about every day. When Lynette handed Bob his first paycheck, his eyes welled up with tears of joy and relief. Finally, he felt productive and alive.

Brent's Story

Brent is a gentle soul. He has large expressive eyes and runs off like a deer if he is surprised. Brent has been diagnosed as autistic since he was a small child. Brent is now a young man. Brent lives in another world, yet he must support himself in this world. Brent supports himself with his job at Candleworks.

One way Brent's autism expresses itself is in the form of repetitive behavior patterns. Rather than seeing this as the disability that had kept him out of the job market, Candleworks saw this as the key to a needed ability at Candleworks. We ship out loads of candles, wrapped in strips cut from large reels of recycled corrugated paper. During the heat of our pre-holiday rush, we literally needed hundreds of thousands of these recycled paper strips. Brent cut and cut and cut with absolute attention, focus and high productivity. He created a small mountain of these paper strips stacked up around his work station. Brent could hardly peek out over the top. Rush orders poured in for these candles, and Brent's mountain started to come down in front of his eyes. With the curiosity of a child, Brent one day followed the trail of all of his candle cover strips into the production room. He totally connected his paper cutting work to the scores of fellow workers wrapping candles with his paper strips. He sat down, and wrapped candles with the paper strips he'd cut. In that moment, Brent connected his place in this community of people. Previously silent, Brent now communicates with many of his co-workers. Brent now has expanded his work repertoire to many other tasks working together with fellow Candleworkers: he centers wick on our electronic candle filler conveyor line. He carefully centers printed labels on many types of candles. Brent now is *part of a community*. This is a breakthrough from his previously private autistic world. Brent found his ability within his disability.

After a busy season of packing thousands and thousands of candles, everyone was ready to relax. A dozen massage therapists donated their time at Thanksgiving to offer a special event at Candleworks: *"A Touch of Gratitude"*. As all the Candleworkers lined up for a therapeutic massage, Brent ran up and jumped on the massage table to be the first. Caring human touch connects us with the community of all life.

Tom's Story

Waking up under the Du Bois Highway Bridge near the Montana state line should not have been that much different from the hundreds of other bridges Tom had slept under during the last seven or eight years. The temperature had dropped severely overnight to 13 degrees above zero. The wind was howling like a mad dog. The chill factor was way below freezing. He fell to sleep as he polished off the last drop left in one of his bottles of MD 20-20 wine. Later that night, the alcohol could not warm him at all anymore. It's probably a good thing that Tom woke up when he did. Tom could easily have frozen to death. He'd messed around too long. Winter set in fast. He should've headed south a month earlier. Looking out through the blinding snow, he could barely see the lights of a distant cafe. Tom made his way to this snowbound sanctuary, hoping they would be open. He pulled back heavy snow to open the door. Tom warmed up his body over several cups of coffee. He set out on the road to hitch a ride to San Antonio, Texas. A close call, he thought, as he headed toward a warmer climate. There had been many close calls in his haphazard, wandering life over the last few years. His wife had been killed in a car wreck eight years earlier in Omaha, Nebraska. They'd raised two beautiful daughters that were now fully grown. Tom's life no longer had a nucleus. He had no responsibilities. Tom hit the road. He slept in railroad yards, jumped trains and hitched rides. Wandering from town to town was fun at first. Then it started taking it's toll. Tom had been severely beaten up many times. After a beating in an alley, he lost his sight in one eye. After another beating, he'd been left for dead. Tom wound up in the emergency ward at the University of California Medical Center for nearly a month. It was slowly dawning on him that this that this free-wheeling endeavor was not his best recourse. Previously, Tom had lived a stable life as a good husband and father. He found himself wanting stability again.

While wandering east on Interstate 80 into Iowa, Tom heard about Candleworks. Some other guys on the road said this was a company that cared about their employees as much as the products they make. "No way", he said. He'd seen it all, and he'd never seen anything like that; a company that treats it's employees like they were part of one big family. "No way", he said again for emphasis. He'd worked for dozens of companies over the last several years. He had no desire to become a permanent employee anywhere. Curiosity pulled him our way. Tom went to Candleworks just to see for himself. Tom's life has been turned totally around. He's now a permanent full time employee. Tom found Candleworks and found himself again.

Chuck's Story

Candleworks has a working partnership with Goodwill Industries. We serve as a work training project to transition disabled workers from Goodwill's sheltered workshops into conventional employment sites. Chuck was the first graduate of this Goodwill training effort. Candleworks hired Chuck as an independent employee, outside of the Goodwill training system. Chuck is now a young man. He doesn't really know his real dad, and probably doesn't want to. Chuck's dad beat him as an infant. This abuse escalated, and after a severe beating, he tossed Chuck into a dumpster.

Loving people found Chuck and took him in as a foster child. From a dumpster to a quality life with dignity is a long trip. Chuck has made that journey with a smile. Chuck always has a helpful attitude at Candleworks. He is assigned from department to department as his help is needed.

At Candleworks, we have another favorite member of our working community who'd also been abused and tossed away as an infant; *Puppers*. Puppers was rescued from the New York City dog pound about four hours before he was scheduled to meet a gassy fate. Puppers is a four-legged, pointy eared, frisky creature who serves as our full time **Ambassador of Affection.** Puppers spends his day circulating among all of our staff. He rests his head from knee to knee until its time to move on to the next person for more petting, and perhaps a left over in the lunch room. At

Candleworks, Chuck is Pupper's caretaker. Chuck always sees that Puppers is fed and watered and he takes him outside the plant for regular walks.

The Goodwill Crew

Our Goodwill crew brings a lot of goodwill to our workplace. A regular visitor to Candleworks often remarks; "if everyone came to their job with the same enthusiasm as this group, we'd have a much more productive society." In spite of very serious mental or physical disabilities, and in many cases a combination of *both*, our goodwill crew make a major contribution to the success of Candleworks. Some of our Goodwill team cannot talk, and some cannot walk. Yet, in the world of Candleworks they communicate their worth, and they move forward in life every day. Our Goodwill workers seldom miss a day of work. Their happy attitude toward each task is infectious. The Goodwill crew add a lot of energy and participation whenever Candleworks has a potluck dinner, a holiday celebration, or we just party for the fun of it. Rose, is one of the Goodwill workers that's been with Candleworks for several years. Everyday, when Rose walks into Candleworks, she always calls out to me:*"Hey, Mike! When's the next party, Mike?"*

Fortunately, there are more and more sheltered workshops for disabled persons. Candleworks is special however, because we fully integrate our very diverse work groups. Everyone works together, no matter what their situation in life. Candleworks reflects the diversity of the human condition. At Candleworks we have a microcosm of the emerging global community. Candleworks is a *working model* for business and community in the 21st Century.

When professional accountants measure the value of a manufacturing business they evaluate the physical and financial assets. They also assign a monetary value to the "goodwill" that the company has built up with the customers in their industry. At Candleworks we have a wealth of Goodwill.

The Candleworks Community

Candleworks keeps growing, so other people now arrive and add their stories to the growing saga of Candleworks. Perhaps some of these additional stories will be told in future editions of this book. Candleworks is a growing organism that changes daily. The life stories included above, however, capture the *diversity* and *essence* of The Candleworks Story. The story continues every day and can never be completely captured in any edition of any book. Life is our story. In our estimation, Candleworks works the way the whole world *should* work. At Candleworks, our goal is to build a world that works for everyone. Candleworks always has an open door. *You are all invited!*

Together, the Candleworks team has faced about every challenge and adversity that the human race has conceived: death, divorce, depression, homelessness despair, alcoholism, drug abuse, prison, suicide, poverty, eviction, serious injury, illness and disability. (So far we haven't faced a tornado, monsoon or a war.)

At Candleworks, we face life's challenges head on and chin up. We've also learned to experience life's joys as a team; a courageous team that knows how to keep on keepin' on when the going is tough. We are a team of survivors. We are ready for all that life presents us. We are getting just as good at accepting the good stuff as we are at solving the bad stuff. Life is a mix of deep joy and sorrow. We know how to experience and love the whole wonderful bundle! Life can be a wild ride. It's important to learn how to let go and ride the waves.

This chapter is the *longest chapter* in this book. That's no accident or mere coincidence. This reflects our *reality*. Candleworks *is* the people that work here. That's why we exist and how we exist. Candleworks doesn't place profit in front of people. We are smart enough however to make a profit *for* our people. Without profit Candleworks would fail. With profit, we can thrive and grow to create more jobs for more people. We profit as a result of our people and principles. The <u>root word</u> of profit is simply *"advance"*.

Bootstrapper's Basic Skill #8: Teamwork is the basis of all success. Success doesn't happen without help. The people involved in your organization are your most important asset. Invest in the self-worth of yourself and your entire team. If an entrepreneur gives everything they've got to their team, the workers give everything they've got to you. No matter what your business, *building your team is your main business.*

Reader's notes:

Who are your most important team members?

family:

friends:

working associates:

Do you have a mentor to provide guidance?

Chapter Nine
Turning Adversity into Advantage
Developing the Winner's Attitude

Success is the result of good judgment.
Good judgment is the result of experience.
Experience is the result of bad judgment.
                              -TONY ROBBINS

Just because you experience a failure doesn't mean you are a failure. Get up, laugh it off, and try again. Real failure only happens if you stop the process of learning from your experiences. *People stop when they get fearful.* Face all fear and move on through it. A problem can be painful, but if we look at how we can learn from it, we can also then apply that learning to profit from the situation. A successful bootstrapper learns how to convert each problem into valuable learning that will create future profit.

The only lessons we learn are the lessons that we actually live. Success is a dynamic *process*, not a destination. The key to success is surviving long enough to use all that we learn from our mistakes. How we manage set backs and problems will determine our ultimate success. If we look at problems as only a drain of energy, it will be just that, and lead to a "quitter's attitude". If we look at problems as challenges to learn from, we'll develop a "winner's attitude". Our very best innovations come from solving problems. Often, the very same problems that could have led to our defeat lead to our breakthroughs, *if we learn from them and keep on going.* Overcome fear and nurture courage.

Starting a bootstrap business takes the same kind of perseverance and discipline as a marathon runner or a long distance swimmer. *No pain, no gain.* Pain is just a signal system that keeps us on track. Imagine that you're a swimmer crossing the English Channel. If fear sets in and you stop, you might just drown. If you're already half way across the channel, it will take just as much time and energy to swim back to your starting point. The fact is it will probably take *more* time and energy, because now the joy of reaching your expected goal no longer fuels your effort. If you are a bootstrapper, its important to *keep on paddling*, even if you hit choppy waters. If you keep your vision high on your real goals, you can keep moving forward. If your vision drops, you'll just see the hard ground as you collapse and fall down.

> *"The game of life is not as much*
> *about holding a good hand*
> *as learning how to play a poor hand well."*
> -H.T. LESLIE

A setback or upset can actually provide *very crucial information* for growth and success if you have the courage to keep up your search for new possibilities.

> *The winners of tomorrow will deal*
> *proactively with chaos,*
> *they will look at the chaos per se*
> *as the source of market advantage,*
> *not as a problem to be gotten around.*
> -TOM PETERS

During our second year of operation, Candleworks accepted an agreement to produce a custom made line of 35 private label aromatherapy candle products for one of the fastest growing specialty retail groups in America: Candleman Stores. Candleman sells only candles and candle accessories. They started with just one store in Minnesota five years ago. They now have almost one hundred stores all over the U.S. and Canada.

This was a great opportunity for Candleworks! If something is good, more of it is probably better, right? That was our thinking. The Candleman group came to us with the opportunity to also manufacture a line of 200 more product varieties, we enthusiastically took the deal. Here is the problem we then encountered; Candleworks already owned adequate manufacturing equipment to produce the line of 35 candle varieties. The line of 200 candle products required new candle molding equipment that we did not yet own. We took the deal on the assumption that we could get the equipment with a pending bank loan.

In April our local bank had made a verbal commitment to Candleworks to put together a S.B.A. loan package of several hundred thousand dollars to finance our rapid growth. With the expectation of this development capital, Candleworks accepted the second deal with Candleman Stores in May. Banks and government agencies are not by nature very entrepreneurial. By September, Candleworks had to face the hard fact that an entrepreneur's sense of time (*very fast*) and a Bank's sense of time (*very slow*) operate in two parallel-non intersecting universes. Banks move slow and cautiously. We were facing the pre-holiday rush to ship the 200 new products varieties to our customers.

The orders for new products were pouring in. There was still no completion of the S.B.A. loan documents with the Bank. Clear communication is necessary for all aspects of bootstrapping. I walked into the bank, and had a meeting with the V.P. of commercial lending to bridge the time gap between banking and entrepreneurial action. Candleworks ships hundreds of packages out monthly by U.P.S. United Parcel has a great marketing slogan: *"moving at the speed of business"*. Now I realized that the opposite was *"moving at the speed of a banker"*.

The local banker told us we did not have proper collateral. Because we'd built our own equipment, it had no defined resale value. I explained to our banker that our enterprise works because of this bootstrapping approach; we make a lot happen with very little resources. We were not going to make many candles however without wax or the necessary equipment to carry out our new custom manufacturing agreement with Candleman Companies. In no uncertain terms, I related to the banker that our bootstraps were now located *somewhere up around our necks*. Our entrepreneurial creative financing had brought us as far as we could go. Our rapid growth now required a healthy line of credit to move forward.

I walked out of the bank without the guaranteed S.B.A financing for the machines, but with an immediate non-guaranteed $100,000 line of credit for our wax and other raw materials. Our candlemakers got busy on two shifts to make up for lost time, making all of the new 200 product varieties *by hand*: without the required machinery.

We were prepared to deliver the goods on this contract through sheer dogged determination. Reality then became evident; the two months time we'd lost waiting for the bank to act was time that could never be recovered. We actually could have kept up the volume required, even making everything with 18th century hand made candle methods; *if we had not lost those two months*. In life, time is more important than money. We can always make more money, *time is irreplaceable*.

We notified this important customer of our dilemma. Candleworks made the difficult decision to defer our opportunity to produce the 200 item product line and concentrate on producing the 35 item product line.

Temporarily, we lost the large contract, but more importantly, we kept this valuable customer. Now several months later, at the time of my writing of this chapter, Candleman Stores are gradually contracting with Candleworks to produce more and more lines of custom products for their stores.

We have now secured an alternative financing source for our candle molding machines. This is 18 months later than we'd originally planned, if the bank could have delivered on their initial verbal commitment. Candleman Stores have again approached us about renegotiating the agreement for the product line of 200 "basic wax" varieties that we suspended last year.

During our 18 month time of delay, disappointment and adversity, Candleworks located a more cost effective source for our candle molding machines. We will now *save* as much money on the purchase of these machines as we would have *profited* if we had made the thousands of products for Candleman Store's "basic wax" line for the entire year! There are two ways to increase profit; increase revenue or decrease cost.

Candleworks has had numerous other experiences where adversity has been converted to major business advantage. We operated our first two years as a grassroots/bootstrap enterprise without adequate investment capital. Undercapitalization was the troll that hid under each bridge to new opportunity.

After the Candleman challenge, when our machinery capitalization was delayed, we encountered another serious setback. We had just secured a private label agreement to make custom aromatherapy candles with our innovative vegetable wax formula for one of the largest natural product distributors in the U.S.

Our first round of production on thousands of these candles hit a very difficult barrier. The braided cotton wick supplier that we worked with shipped us 10,000 units of pre-tabbed wick. This wick was all labeled with the correct code for the size of candle in production. The actual wick delivered was a slightly smaller wick that had been *mislabeled* at the wick factory. There are literally hundreds of sizes and types of wick. Without the proper wick, the candle will not burn properly. Depending on the size of the candle, the wick must be large enough to consume the pool of molten wax that is created by the candle flame. A wick that is too small will literally be drowned in the pool of wax that it's flame creates. As a result we delivered 10,000 candles that self-extinguished. One of the necessary tools of bootstrapping is humor. We recalled that the root meaning humor means *fluid*. Humor actually creates flexibility. Laugh and you can *bend*. Get tense, stressed out, rigid and you *break*. Humor is a required survival tool for all bootstrappers. It's important to see the absurdity in your adversity. What could be more absurd than a candle that will not burn! Do you laugh or cry? We chose to laugh, loosen up, get busy and confront the adversity.

Our self-extinguishing candle problem originated with our wick supplier. When this error was discovered, we did not waste one word making an excuse to our customer that the problem was someone else's fault. Candleworks accepted full responsibility for the situation. We called back 10,000 candles with the faulty wick. We re-made them and preserved our relationship with this very important customer. We took a short term sacrifice to preserve our long term good. Problems do happen. The most important thing is to communicate directly with all parties involved, accept responsibility and solve them. This major adversity, painful as it was, led to innovation and further business advantage:

1. We now include in our quality control procedures, pre-testing and burn tests of each shipment of wick. This way we *verify* that the wick shipped to us is the actual wick that we ordered, and the wick is the type that the product code stamped on the box says that it is.

2. Because of the unreliable labeling procedures of our former wick supplier, we set out on a global search for the *very best wick we could find*. Candleworks found a new wick manufacturer in Germany that had started production one month after the faulty wick was delivered to us. This German wick is the finest wick available anywhere in the world. This company didn't even exist when our problem took place. Without our

problem, however, we would not have been actively looking for them. This alternative source has proven to be far superior. As a result of the problem, all of our candles now perform much better. A quality problem led us to a major quality improvement in all products that we now manufacture.

Another example of converting adversity to advantage came when our growth cycle hit an exponential wave. It's the common industry standard for a manufacturer to finance all material, production and labor costs up front. Customers are billed 30 days after delivery. Fast growth requires larger and larger sources of working capital to fund the expanding business.

Before we found a bank who would set up an adequate line of credit for supplies and labor during production, we regularly hit the entrepreneurial brick wall called *undercapitalization*. A bootstrapper becomes as agile as an athlete. When you hit a brick wall, you climb over it, do a running high jump, pole vault over it, build a door through it or dig a tunnel under it.

Candleworks' market niche is making private label, custom scented aromatic candles. We work with the foremost perfumers and fragrance houses in the world to develop our distinctive aroma blends. During one of our rapid growth cycles, we fell 60 days behind with our payments to our primary fragrance manufacturer. Right in the middle of a busy production season, they cut off our credit, and required cash on delivery. Fragrance oils are the single most expensive component in our manufacturing process. We did not have advance working capital to pay C.O.D. up front.

Candleworks was gaining growing recognition in the national market. Smaller, entrepreneurial fragrance manufacturers started contacting us, just as we hit this barrier in our production. We tested fragrance oils from several smaller companies. We found one that offered a superior product at a 15% cost savings compared with the large manufacturer that refused to be flexible with our payment plan. We now save 15% on all fragrance oil purchases. We directed this 15% savings into payments on our bill with the old supplier; our new supplier gives us the credit we need to operate efficiently. Candleworks tries to be as flexible as we reasonably can be with any of our small start-up entrepreneurial customers. We know how it feels to be on the other side of the fence. The small struggling bootstrapper of today may be the industry giant in five years. We work with other start-up entrepreneurs, so we can grow along with them. By networking with other bootstrapping entrepreneurs, we can foster each other's development and growth.

If a door closes, don't sit around for a moment and mope. Leap through the nearest window. Bootstrappers become experts at making lemonade out of lemons. This is a crucial survival skill. An entrepreneur is by nature an optimist. This is the prime trait that can open the door to success; it is also the trait that leads to the downfall of many entrepreneurial ventures. The most common cause of the failure of a business is growth that comes too rapidly. Balance and timing are crucial. If your entrepreneurial enterprise does fail, it's important to evaluate what you learned and try again. Very few bootstrappers hit a home run the first time they get out on the field. If you do trip and fall, get up and try again. Never, ever give up on yourself.

Rather than blind optimism, we learn to apply practical optimism bolstered by very hard work. Entrepreneurs are in a different class than simple visionaries and dreamers. Entrepreneurs have dreams and vision, but this is balanced with a solid grasp of reality. Bootstrappers keep their eyes on the highest sky, and their feet planted firmly on the ground. An idle dreamer is stopped by the first obstacle in the real world. They just move on to a new fantasy. A bootstrapper is a visionary with a gut full of intestinal fortitude, perseverance and chutzpah. Candleworks growth has been very challenging. We've arrived at many strategic crossroads in the development of this business where it would have been much easier to quit than to persevere and move forward.

Recently, Candleworks was recognized with the annual "Courage and Perseverance Award" at the National "Never Fear, Never Quit" Conference organized each year by author, business consultant and motivational speaker, Joe Tye. Candleworks was selected for this honor because every day we live the principles presented in Joe Tye's best known book, *"Never Fear, Never Quit"*

> *"The only place where success comes before work is in a dictionary."*
> -VIDAL SASSOON

If you want the rainbow, you've gotta go through the rain. Never fear, never quit, follow your gut instinct.

> *If opportunity doesn't knock, build a door."*
> -MILTON BERLE

> *"Obstacles are what we see when we take our eyes off of our goal"*
> - E. JOSEPH COSSMAN

In the New Testament we find a verse:*"The evil of the day is sufficient there of".* Jesus spoke these words like a seasoned entrepreneur. This principle is a very important survival tool for entrepreneurs. Only deal with what you can in any one day. A bootstrapper is sometimes confronted by so many challenges and barriers, that there is only one way to work through them; *one at a time.* Make a list of the challenges. This gets them out of your head and on paper. Now your mind is free to find solutions one problem at a time.

Many entrepreneurs are always trying to drain the swamp, while surrounded with chomping crocodiles.

Tame, tackle, or terminate each crocodile one at a time. Draining the swamp then becomes much simpler.

Make a <u>list</u> of challenges to solve each day. Do your damnedest to shorten the list. Then forget about it and go home to play, love, laugh, rest. You'll come back swinging with both fists early the next morning. Only deal with emotionally and physically what you can do *in one day of hard work.* Then leave your work and *let go of all the remaining problems.* You don't even need to remember the problems when you leave your work. Your problems, the bills, all unmet goals *will come looking for you the next day.* Follow this plan, and you can meet each opposing force fresh and feisty, rather than fatigued and fearful.

A bootstrapper has one skill that most people don't have; they are exceptional problem solvers. A bootstrapper learns that by not giving in to doubt and worry, you can keep the calm mental state required for a sharp mind that will find the solutions you need.

Problems are solved much more readily if they are identified, separated, prioritized and then tackled one at a time. This makes your problems manageable, rather than an unmanageable tangle of worry, fear and stress.

Almost all bootstrappers immediately find themselves surrounded by an unexpected wealth; a wealth of challenges, problems and adversity. Be grateful for this wealth. Each adversity is a priceless teacher. Face each one fearlessly, and you will be on your way to earning your **M.B.A.** (Master of Business Adversity).

> *An executive is someone who makes decisions, and is right once in a while.*
> -ELBERT HUBBARD

Reasoned, yet lighting quick decision making is another key survival tool of the bootstrapper. As an entrepreneur, you cannot avoid making decisions. Every decision avoided is a decision already made by default. Inaction is always riskier than bold action. In the history of military strategy, decisive, bold action leads to victory. In war and life, hesitation is death.

Fortune assists the bold.
-VIRGIL

Whatever you lack in money, expertise or connections can be replaced with courage. Courage unlocks the vaults of Providence. After lots of struggle, our work began to gain a lot of recognition. Regional and national print and broadcast media came and documented our project. Candleworks has been featured on PBS, CBS, Success Magazine and a score of local newspapers.

Candleworks was named Business of the Year by the Human Rights Commission of our local government.

We were invited to a National Symposium of Social Entrepreneurs in Washington D.C. sponsored by American Express, S.O.S. "Charge Against Hunger".

At the National Conference of Mayors, President Clinton presented Candleworks with the "Best Practice" award from the Federal office of Housing and Urban Development (H.U.D.)

Rotary International named the Candleworks founders to the International Paul Harris Fellowship for humanitarian service.

At the national "Never Fear, Never Quit" conference, Candleworks was presented the annual "Courage and Perseverance Award".

Recently Candleworks was nominated for a "Blue Chip Enterprise Award" to recognize business initiative.

Candleworks was nominated for the U.S. Small Business Administration's "Business of the Year Award" to recognize our *welfare to work* leadership efforts.

We hope our experience inspires other bootstrappers everywhere. Seek challenges. Learn from adversity. Never let fear defeat you. Don't quit 'til you win. If you do loose a round, keep getting back into the fight 'til you win. *Some of the greatest success stories in history are the result of spectacular first failures:*

*Macy went bankrupt eleven times trying to launch the novel notion of a "Department Store". Macy's is now a legend of both retail marketing and popular myth, as the "Miracle on 34th Street."

*Legendary basketball great, Michael Jordan was cut from his Junior High team. He worked all the harder. He worked his way to the very top of his game.

*Abraham Lincoln was defeated a dozen times before he finally won his first office at the bootstrap level of local politics. He then bootstrapped all the way to the top to become the greatest President in our history.

*Colonel Sanders traveled all over the South trying to market his secret blend of spices to successful restaurant operators. He was rejected over 1000 times! He finally set up his own tiny chicken stand in desperation. At age 65, Colonel Sanders started one of the most successful entrepreneurial ventures in history. Colonel Sanders stands as proof of the bootstrapper's adage: *"it's never too late to become what you might have become."* It's never too late to start, but it's always too soon to quit.

A real bootstrapper is never too old, never too poor, never too disadvantaged, never too disabled, never too misunderstood to make their lasting mark in the world. The Bootstrapper's Hall of Fame is filled with endless walls hung with portraits of people who failed and failed and just would not quit until they won. They all knew that success was their destiny, even if it took most of their life to finally convince the rest of the world of that obvious fact. As long as you are breathing and have a heart beat, you aren't defeated. Whatever doesn't kill you, will just make you stronger. After a fall, get up, laugh a little, and keep on going.

Bootstrapper's Basic Skill #9: Make adversity your ally. Within every problem lie unclaimed jewels of opportunity. Become a master at finding this value. Find the absurdity in all adversity. Keep laughing 'til you win.

Reader's notes:

What do you consider the grandest failure or greatest adversity you've ever faced?

What did you learn from this adversity or failure?

What barrier or adversity is blocking the path to your life's mission and your greatest goal right now?

What action step can you take today to start overcoming this barrier or adversity?

Chapter Ten
Spiritual Entrepreneurship
"The Way of the Bootstrapper"

The highest reward for a person's work is not what they get for it, but what they become by it.
-JOHN RUSKIN

Candleworks rapid growth required more and more capital for larger and larger deliveries of raw material so that we could produce larger and larger orders. In the Spring of 1997 we encountered our most challenging cash crisis ever. Rapid production leading up to the Holiday retail season during the 4th quarter of 1996 required payroll of a quarter of a million dollars in just 6 months. We were facing a $42,000 payroll withholding deposit to the IRS. Our customers owed us $100,000, but the Feds wanted cash *now*.

At this point, when it looked like the door was about to shut on Candleworks, the door opened and an "angel" walked in. In circles of working entrepreneurs, the term "angel" refers to a benevolent investor that shows up with needed capital just as the bootstrapping business encounters a major barrier. Angels do step in where others fear to tread.

An entrepreneur requires the same physical and mental traits as a warrior: passion, commitment, courage and undaunted endurance. Bootstrapping separates the men from the boys and the girls from the strong hearted women. Courage is one of the key traits of the bootstrapping entrepreneur. Courage is defined as taking decisive action *in spite of fear*. Courage provides the motivation to keep on moving through the initial stages of fear, doubt and challenge on your road to success. Faith keeps alive the belief in the vision that sometimes only the bootstrapper can see. Your vision keeps you forging forward on thin air; until the solid ground of success gradually begins to meet the persistent tread of your feet.

> *You may be disappointed if you fail,*
> *but you will be doomed if you don't try.*
> —BEVERLY SILS

Nothing in the world can take the place of persistence: Talent will not; nothing is more common than unsuccessful men with great talent. Genius will not: unrewarded genius is almost a proverb. Education will not: the world is full of educated derelicts. Persistence and determination alone are omnipotent.
—CALVIN COOLIDGE

Of every ten new business ventures that start up, only two or three survive and thrive. Persistence and determination, and the courage to *never quit* are the final determining factors for success. A breakthrough success often comes directly after adversity that would make most people give up. Persistence is very crucial.

Success is more attitude than aptitude.

True entrepreneurship is akin to the martial arts; we *re-direct* challenging forces that come at us into productive, positive channels. We direct the forces of the world through our own *attitude, intention* and *action*.

> Depending on the circumstances,
> You should be hard as a diamond,
> flexible as a willow,
> smooth flowing like water,
> or as empty as space.
> —MORIHEI UESHIBA

An entrepreneur must be flexible. If one door closes, spin quickly and survey every direction for the very next opening for your development, growth and success. Life and success abound with paradox.

> "Move like a beam of light,
> Fly like lightning,
> Strike like thunder,
> Whirl in circles around a stable center.
> -MORIHEI UESHIBA

A rather obscure tradition in martial arts and the Eastern mind is referred to as **"Thick Face/Black Heart"**. It's a bit challenging to describe this mind set to a Western mind, but an understanding of "Thick Face/Black Heart is essential to walk the "Way of the Bootstrapper".

A Thick Face/Black Heart practitioner is like a wolf in the deepest woods. Austere, silent, an outsider with a connection to no one, yet with a vital connection to everything. There is only one species that's more biologically successful than the wolf; humans. A wolf is attuned to natural law, and thus survives and thrives. Thick Face/Black Heart is nature's basic law.

First, Thick Face means that you are strong to the outside world, your face is as firm and set as your mind. No amount of doubt, ridicule or attack from the outside world will change the countenance of your face or the composure of your mind. A practitioner of Thick Face does not need to save face, or be respected, admired or even accepted by the people around them. The source of their self esteem is a deep *inner* well. It does not depend on praise from any outside source. Every great innovator in human civilization has first been greeted with ridicule and disdain by others.

"Black Heart" is an even more challenging concept to describe to Western minds. A practitioner of "Black Heart" answers to his own heart and natural law rather than social expectation and moral convention. Sometimes it appears they are aloof and arrogant. Deep inside, however, they have a deep love that is far beyond mere displays of kindness. Thick Face/Black Heart practitioners are an enigma, a deep paradox.

An ancient Zen parable describes the Thick Face/Black Heart state of mind: *A group of holy monks lived in the woods near a town. They were ascetics that lived with no money, very little food, and wandered the woods with no permanent home. One monk, an odd sort of fellow, smiled and laughed when the other ascetics were austere and serious. The other monks spent every waking hour in devout prayer. The odd monk played with the animals of the forest and the little children that curiously wandered into their camp. One day, the odd monk started painting the beauty he saw in the world. The ascetics reprimanded him and told him he should instead pray and meditate.*

With "Thick Face", their criticism and disdain of him went unheeded, like water off of a duck's back. The monk then started wandering into the town and mixing with people. The merchants of the town were amazed at the exquisite paintings he carried. The merchants purchased the monk's fine paintings. The odd monk's money pouch grew fatter and fatter to the horror of the other monks. A vow of poverty was central to their faith, and here this "black hearted" sinner was among them. In their critical eye, he was unholy and soiled by the world and money.

The odd monk joyously continued in his wayward path. The community of monks were ready to expel this infidel from their life. A great drought came and persisted. The tiny patches of corn and paddies of rice the monks tended in the woods shriveled. A great famine came. The holy monks were all near death. The odd monk unlaced his bursting bag of money saved from all the paintings he had sold to the merchants in the town. He took his small fortune and traded it with the merchants for giant bundles of food and provisions. He then went back to his community of monks. He fed them all and saved their lives.

The heart of such a person is only black to the outside view of small minded moralists. Inside, their heart is wrought of pure, polished gold, tempered by life's fire. Jesus actually practiced Thick Face/Black Heart. He had a "Thick Face" non-concern about how the religious authorities viewed him. He answered to a higher power, and not society. He stated that "he was no respecter of persons". Jesus constantly broke the moral and legal codes of his day and lived by the Law of Love. His daily companions were the rejected of the world; prostitutes, ruffians, commoners, "the unclean". The moral and holy Pharisees, the upholders of every letter of the law considered Jesus their nemesis.

The most clear contemporary portrayal of a "Thick Face/Black Heart" state of mind in Western culture is Oscar Shindler in Spielberg's astounding movie, *Shindler's List*. At first impression, Shindler is amoral, a manipulator, a womanizer, a social chameleon, a profiteer; yet he is the courageous instrument of life and salvation for concentration camp victims during the Holocaust. Oscar Shindler's life is a paradox.

Oscar Shindler is indeed a bootstrapper, portrayed by one of the most successful bootstrappers of our era, Steven Spielberg. To become a filmaker, Spielberg put into practice a very important principle of "The Way of The Bootstrapper": **The Law of Assumption.** This law means that you just have the courage to *assume* your role in the world. You do not ask for permission or approval, you just step in, assume your position and get busy. You do not need a degree, a license, etc. Your value in the world is self defined and divinely graced.

Spielberg never went to a prestigious film school at a lofty university. He started with no money and no professional connections. As a teenager, he just wandered into the sets of major Hollywood studios with his own hand held camera. He became a squatter in an abandoned trailer on a studio backlot. He'd walk around, shooting any action he could find. A quiet, yet friendly youth, he befriended the stage hands, technicians and people who could let him into any back door of the studio complex. People got to know the kid. People came to like the him. He bootstrapped his way up through low status television directing gigs, on into feature films, directing, producing, literally *assuming* his way to the very top of an extremely competitive industry.

The *Way of the Bootstrapper* is akin to the *Way of the Warrior* of traditional indigenous tribal peoples. The Latin word for profit simply translates "to advance". A warrior advances against all odds, with courage and determination. The action of advance, creates the profit.

"Spirituality cannot be something a person
toys with, a little compartment of their lives.
It must be at the core,
in a way that effects every part of their lives."
-STEVEN COVEY

There is immense power in our intention and our vision. What we visualize is what we get. The stronger our vision, the more direct is our path to our goal.

If you can dream it, you can do it.
-WALT DISNEY

By believing passionately in something
that still does not exist, we create it.
The non-existent is whatever we have
not yet sufficiently desired.
-NIKOS KAZANTZAKIS

During the first struggling months of Candleworks in New York City, our family lived in a cramped two bedroom apartment. *All we had was vision* to build our business with. We had no capital. The only room for sleeping was in a cramped loft that was just two feet from the ceiling. I wrote a simple verse to voice our vision and taped it to the ceiling in front of my view:

I see the clear white light of **one** candle.
I see the bright light of hundreds of candles.
I see the expanding light of thousands of candles.
I see the exquisite light of millions of candles.
I see an expanding infinity of luminous candles.
I see the **one** great infinite light. I *am* that light.

Each morning as I awakened, I read this verse above me. Each night as I fell into bed, sometimes very tired from 16 hour work days, this verse was my last thoughtful meditation as I accepted the renewal of sleep. From day one, this simple **vision of light** has guided every day of the growth of Candleworks. This is also a very clear vision of life's growth and expansion.

In our era, the road to holiness necessarily passes through the world of action.
-DAG HAMMARSKJOLD (former U.N. Secretary General)

There are more mystics in the board rooms of businesses with bootstrap roots, than in all of the monasteries of all of the religions of the earth. Entrepreneurs have a light in the eye. A vitality. A creativity and passion that other entrepreneurs recognize in a silent, universal bond of unity. Faith is an absolute necessity for the bootstrapper. An entrepreneur without faith is like a car without gas. Faith is literally trust in the unseen level of reality.

<u>Making something from nothing</u> is the spiritual discipline of the bootstrapper. Jesus, then is the ultimate entrepreneur of all history. In the Gospel of Matthew, Verse 14, a huge crowd has gathered to hear Jesus teach. Jesus instructs his disciples to feed the entire multitude. The disciples protest that they only have five loaves of bread and two fish. Jesus breaks the bread, and the fish *as he looks to heaven*. Five thousand people line up to be fed. Now you might think, five thousand! A captive market. If this Jesus

fellow is a real entrepreneur, he's got humanity's first opportunity to set up flashy double Golden Arches and let fast food history begin. Jesus, however, instructs his disciples to *give the food away.* 5,000 people are fed. The disciples then gather in baskets and baskets of <u>left-overs</u>. He not only created *principal,* the left overs were a demonstration of *interest!* (grace) Many conventional businessmen would think that Jesus let a major sales opportunity just pass by. Bona fide entrepreneurs *know the reality*: the more you give, the more you receive. In fact, the effects of those first loaves and fishes the Entrepreneur from Galilee gave away are *still expanding* two thousand years later.

An entrepreneur's motivation is to create something from nothing; then get their creation into circulation for growth and human benefit. A lot of entrepreneurs are actually bored with counting all the money produced from their ventures. They hire accountants to take care of that. The goal for most entrepreneurs is the <u>creative act itself</u>. Making money is simply a *by-product* of this creativity. Spielberg never set out to make money, *he makes movies.* Money is a by-product, not the product of the bootstrappers action and entrepreneurial spirit.

According to Matthew in the gospel story told above, directly after this abundance of supply is produced from nothing, Jesus retreats to a quiet mountain to *acknowledge God.* In this gospel story are the <u>two keys</u> for the Way of the Entrepreneur:

1. When faced with the appearance of a shortage of supply, *turn to heaven for your supply.*

2. After abundance is manifest in the material world, always *retreat with gratitude* to your spiritual source.

These <u>two simple steps</u> keep the creative flow of entrepreneurial energy moving freely in your life.

A strong spiritual foundation is the very basis of an entrepreneur's courage and perseverance. If we perceive our employees, customers, bankers and even our competitors as part of *one whole spiritual system*, then there is no fear to inhibit our success. In love, their is no fear. Faith and love are the key resources with which a bootstrapper builds success.

Success can not just be measured by the size of an entrepreneur's bank account or the value of their physical assets. The real measure of success is the *value* that we add to ourselves, our world and those that work with us in our enterprise. An entrepreneur increases their own self-esteem through creative, fulfilling activity. They increase the esteem of family, peers, the community. They earn the respect and esteem of those they create employment and growth opportunities for. An entrepreneur often adds to the quality of life through advancement of medicine, technology or other human benefit. An entrepreneur opens up the flow of financial prosperity of all those that work for and with them.

All successful entrepreneurs discover how to create something of value that will live on after they die. In this way, they achieve immortality. By developing talented successors in your enterprise, something of value continues on in the world after your life; a body of new knowledge, a new invention that continues to improve the lives of others for years to come. A legacy for your family can provide the means for continued creativity and success for generations. A financial endowment to a university or cultural institution is often included in the legacy of an entrepreneur.

All human advancement either directly, or indirectly has come through the channels of entrepreneurial effort. Bootstrappers keep the wheels turning. They are the builders of life's evolution. There are entrepreneurs in every field of human endeavor. Find the work that you love to do, and get busy now.

Since they start with no bounty of physical resources, a bootstrapper *of necessity*, taps into an infinite bounty of spiritual resources. In the open expanse of nothingness, you find the source of everything *inside* yourself. The source of all prosperity is within you.

Take heart, have courage, keep your vision clear. Step into the "Way of the Bootstrapper". You will never be the same. The world will never be the same.

Bootstrapper's Basic Skill #10: Build your work on a strong spiritual foundation. Fearless faith will get you through all obstacles placed in your path.

> *Except the Lord build the house,*
> *they labour in vain that build it.*
> **Psalm 127**

Reader's notes:

How do you connect with your own inner Source?

How can you deepen this connection to your Source?

How can you assist all of your co-workers to build this connection to their inner source?

Who's the most influential spiritual mentor in your life?

How can you express your deepest spiritual nature in your everyday life?

Chapter Eleven
Finding Your Balance
Building a Strong Foundation

A major challenge for most entrepreneurial ventures is discovering how to make the transition to a stable, mature, strong and lasting organization with a firm foundation. What is the legacy your life will create?

An equal challenge is for the bootstrapping entrepreneur to find ways to maintain a balanced lifestyle that gives equal importance to family, self and society as to the bootstrap venture. If your dream venture becomes all-consuming of your time and energy, your dream may become your nightmare.

The founding bootstrapper is usually an extreme individualist. An iconoclast that has challenged the dominant social, political or economic system, must eventually find creative ways to integrate with that system without losing their zeal and identity.

The bootstrapper starts out as a "jack of all trades" through sheer necessity. There are usually no funds in start up organizations for adequate support staff. After a bootstrapper has done everything for and by themselves for several years, it's a challenge to then learn how to delegate key tasks to key individuals.

If an entrepreneurial organization is to grow, it must become larger than the founding bootstrapper. The key to effective delegation is *trust*. The start-up bootstrapper must eventually recruit the kind of people that they can entrust important aspects of the operation to: an accountant or business manager, perhaps marketing or P.R. people, and co-managers to operate growing divisions of the organization.

The key to trust is finding those people that share deeply in your *original vision* and *core values*. This vision and these core values will guide these new delegate's decisions and implementation of new projects. Your associates' values and vision will guide them, just like your values and vision as the founding bootstrapper have guided you.

If it takes a bootstrapper sixteen hours a day to carry out the management functions of a small start up organization; the need will double to 32 man-hours to carry out these same functions at some point in the venture's growth. Since 32 hours is impossible to squeeze out of a 24 hour day, the bootstrapper must learn to delegate some functions to trusted associates. When management functions grow to the point where 48, 60, 72 man-hours and more are required each day, then a trusted management team must be built.

Some passionate bootstrappers never learn this. They work far beyond their physical, emotional and psychological limits. The inevitable result of such a path is terminal burn-out of you or your organization.

Successful bootstrappers learn that their own physical, spiritual and mental energy is the engine that motivates the entrepreneurial venture. It's imperative to learn what you need to do to re-charge this energy on a very regular basis. Perhaps stopping your fast-paced work every 3 or 4 hours to take a walk or meditate can be a tool to accomplish this. Some relaxation time with family and friends where work is not considered or discussed is very important. Perhaps activities in sports, the arts or other interests outside of your bootstrap venture can regenerate your inner batteries. Once in a while a sabbatical or vacation completely away from your work can create a deep new reservoir of creative ideas, motivation and expanded personal energy.

Many entrepreneurs, who at one time had been serious workaholics, report that when they learn to take time to create this balance in their personal life, they actually produce more successful results in less hours!

An entrepreneur's *personal enthusiasm* is their most reliable barometer of impending burnout. If your enthusiasm starts to wane, you are getting out of balance and wandering off track. Concentrate on doing what you are good at. Put your energy into what you love. The classic entrepreneurial personality gets their buzz from the big picture; seeing their vision come into reality. Often times, they fall short in daily details like book keeping and record filing. Get help with all tasks that do not excite you. These tasks *will excite other personality types.* A fine set of balanced books has all the harmony of an exquisite symphony to an accountant that loves their work. Do the work you love, and find people who love all of the other necessary tasks to keep your organization efficient. Enthusiasm is the fuel that will keep your organization vital. Enthusiasm is a Greek word that literally translates as *"god within"*. Keep that fire in your heart burning at full force, and you will be invincible. Enthusiasm is a magnet that will draw in the help you need. People are hungry to enter into a labor of love.

When your bootstrap organization grows faster than the available cash resources to hire professional help, you can begin to distribute some of the responsibility for research, planning and decision making by forming a voluntary advisory board. Your advisory board should be made up of other like-minded people. Seek out successful retired entrepreneurs, community leaders, local experts or other resource people. If you have a nearby university you can often arrange for excellent help with specific projects and tasks from student interns. Some internship programs require that you pay a small amount, and other internships are provided without cost.

When your organization gets to the point where you do hire key management staff to grow the bootstrap venture, it's really important to recruit staff on an equal basis of their core values and vision as well as their specific professional or technical skills.

In addition to effective selection of key management staff, regular staff training and occasional off-site retreats for all participants in your organization can provide an excellent means to instill and deepen your original core vision and values throughout the entire body politic. It's just as important to build and strengthen the values and vision of all the people in your organization as it is to deliver whatever your specific product or service is. Your original vision and work then has a much longer life than just your own.

Most of the successful and enduring business, arts, social, religious and educational institutions were actually started several generations ago by bootstrappers just like you. All great institutions are the extended shadow of a risk taking pioneer. That's the exciting thing about creating an entrepreneurial venture; you're creating something vital with a life of its own. Bootstrapping is an act of creation. What long term legacy will your life create? Start small, think big. Get started with what you have. *Light one candle!* The reflection of that light will shine through all time.

Real success cannot be measured simply in financial terms. Real success includes successful personal adjustment and emotional health. Real success includes the health and welfare of your family and community. Real success must include *balance, health and joy.*

Bootstrapper's Basic Skill #11: Live a balanced life. Entrepreneurs who keep a lively interest in health, family, community, sports and the arts thrive. A person who lives a healthy, balanced life will have the energy to create and produce in five hours what a burned out workaholic can in fifteen hours.

Reader's notes:

What's most important to me in addition to my bootstrap venture or my career goals?

Do I spend an equal balance of my time on these other areas of priority and value?

How can I organize my life to maintain and nurture these other important areas of my life?

When was the last time that you experienced the same kind of joy and enthusiasm that you did as a child?

What kind of activity really excites you? How can you start to build a career or business based on this special activity that you love?

Chapter Twelve
Training, Support, Going Global

One of the legacies that I wish to provide is a well defined path for future bootstrappers to trod. I want every possible symphony to be composed, every masterpiece to be painted, every business idea to be pursued and every new vision to be realized. That's the purpose of this book; to stimulate creative action in every field of human endeavor.

In order for the thousands of bootstrappers who read this book to be successful, a lot of support will be needed. By definition, bootstrappers are creating something new, with very little resources. Pioneers need a trail to follow, and companions to travel with.

You will be like salmon swimming upstream to plant fertile new ideas. The force of the whole stream will be working against you. If you are a bona fide bootstrapper, rather than an idle dreamer, this counter force will strengthen you, deepen your resolve and clarify your vision. It will not be easy though.

The only way that salmon sense how to swim upstream is because of the pathways clearly defined by the struggle of all the generations of salmon that have preceded them. **This book is to share this way.**

<u>Now let's get you started on your own bootstrap path:</u>
The essential tool of bootstrapping is *immediate decisive action.* Start today toward your goal with whatever resources, courage and energy you can muster. The opposite of the bootstrapper's state of mind is procrastination. There is no procrastination allowed in the ranks of the bootstrappers' boot camp. Let's get you motivated into action at this very moment. Here's your first **<u>Short Course in Bootstrap Basics:</u>**

A Short Course in Bootstrap Basics

The 5 principles of bootstrap success:

SELF-WORTH, INVESTMENT, STRATEGY, ACTION, MEASUREMENT

If you think you have nothing with which to start a business, or realize your dream goals, then *think again*. Discover the wealth you do have: You are your most valuable asset. You're your own source of wealth.

1. Your own self-worth is the seed of all future wealth.

a. Personal Value Inventory; know your own value.

These are the **key personal values** that will create entrepreneurial success. Measure your present value. Circle the **present value** of your personal inventory.
1 is the minimum measure, **10** is the maximum.

Courage	1	2	3	4	5	6	7	8	9	10
Creativity	1	2	3	4	5	6	7	8	9	10
Perseverance	1	2	3	4	5	6	7	8	9	10
Flexibility	1	2	3	4	5	6	7	8	9	10
Passion	1	2	3	4	5	6	7	8	9	10
Commitment	1	2	3	4	5	6	7	8	9	10
Work Ethic	1	2	3	4	5	6	7	8	9	10
Love	1	2	3	4	5	6	7	8	9	10
Energy	1	2	3	4	5	6	7	8	9	10
Spirituality	1	2	3	4	5	6	7	8	9	10

b. Creative Capital Assessment
   (ideas, experience, knowledge, community networks)

Internal Capital (the basis of your product or service)

My three most creative ideas are:
1.
2.
3.

Idea translates as the root I (*from*) Dea (*God*) Ideas, are your basic capital, direct for the Main Source. The more you respect your ideas and *act on them*, the more ideas you'll have flowing from this vast inner source.

My three most valuable life experiences are:
1.

2.

3.

Your own direct life experience is your most effective teacher. **A lesson lived is a lesson learned.**

My three other most important sources of knowledge:
1.

2.

3.

External Capital: Networks and Connections
(Your present networks are the basis of your market)
My three most important personal networks are:
1.

2.

3.
(Your past jobs, church, school groups, clubs, family associations, etc. are the basis of your networks.)

Your personal value inventory and creative capital is the wealth that you <u>now possess</u> to create your new enterprise.

The next step is investing in this personal wealth; to *increase* it's value on an upward growing curve.

2. <u>Investment</u>

Invest in your personal worth, and you open the vault to unlimited growth of your value. You can invest in yourself through education, training, mentoring, building networks of connection, reading, travel and new experience. *Personal growth pays the highest interest.* There are no better investments than you.

My personal investment plan for the next 6 months:
1. (education and training plans)

2. (new networks to build and participate in)

3. (new life experience to seek out and get involved in)

3. <u>Strategy:</u> (strategy includes *mission* and *action*)

The <u>mission statement</u> of Candleworks is: *To develop an innovative business enterprise that generates creative resources to activate personal, community and global transformation to a life based on love rather than fear.*

a. My personal mission statement for my own life is:

Have your profit center be the same as your *passion center.* Do what you love, and you will do it very well. Goals that advance your mission will be imbued with passion. Work on one key goal at a time. Build new success from each prior success. Your completed goals provide the foundation on which to build future goals.

My one year plan:

b. My Priority Goal for the next 3 months:

c. My Priority Goal for the second 3 months:

d. My Priority Goal for the third 3 months:

e. My Priority Goal for the fourth 3 months:

4. Action

Audacious, grand scale goals are possible if we break them down into small steps that we can schedule daily.

My personal plan of action to implement my mission:

My action steps for today: *(make a list each day)*
1.
2.
3.
4.
5.

My action steps for the week: *(make a list each week)*
1.
2.
3.
4.
5.

My action steps for the month   *(make a list each month)*

1.
2.
3.
4.
5.

My action steps for this year:
1.
2.
3.
4.
5.

Bold action is what separates effective bootstrappers from idle dreamers. *Decisive action generates energy.*

5. Measurement
Unless there is measure, there is no movement.

1. **Criteria;** Create a definite *unit of measure:* cash made, products produced, services rendered, people served, projects completed, etc.

My unit of measure is :_____

2. **Deadline**
(Establish your realistic target date of completion.)
Completion Date: _____

MY PLAN IS MY DREAM WITH A DEADLINE.
NO DEAL IS DEFINITE WITHOUT A CONTRACT.

MY CONTRACT WITH MYSELF:

<u>Fill in the blanks:</u>

I will complete:
_____
_____
(define this with your unit of measurement)

by this date_____

Signed:_____

Start date:_____

REMEMBER, YOUR PROJECT PLAN
IS YOUR DREAM WITH A DEADLINE.

Please send a copy of your contract to the author of this book at P.O. Box 975, Iowa City, Iowa 52244. I will send you a post card on your stated date of completion.

Now you can get on your way down the bootstrap path.

LIGHT ONE CANDLE!

A journey of a thousand miles starts with a single step. Enjoy the trip. That way you will love the destination.

If you can dream it, you can do it.
-WALT DISNEY

You will need other tools, guidance and support to follow through with your bootstrap dream. Here are some ways that you can get these <u>important resources:</u>

1. Participate with seasoned and start up bootstrappers in the **Bootstrappers' Network**. This is the very best way to share ideas, support and connections with other entrepreneurs on the bootstrap path. *Get connected.*

The primary communication tool of the Bootstrappers' Network is our Network Newsletter: BOOTSTRAPPING. BOOTSTRAPPING is an informative and entertaining publication. This quarterly newsletter provides an inspiring profile of a successful bootstrap entrepreneur in each issue. Letters from member bootstrappers with specific questions are answered with common sense advice. This bootstrapper's newsletter provides you with vital information that you will not find in any conventional business magazine. This publication is *by, for and about* bootstrapping entrepreneurs working on their dream.

To subscribe to your Bootstrapper's Newsletter, send $24 to Innovation Press, P.O.Box 975, Iowa City, Ia. 52244 *All subscribers are members of the Bootstrap Network.*

2. The University of Real Life Experience
If you have a dynamic idea that you're ready to bootstrap, our Network provides two very valuable education opportunities to prepare you for success:

A. Bootstrapper's Bootcamp, Basic Training
Spend a weekend in the trenches with seasoned entrepreneurs. You'll gain strategy, tools and motivation to launch your bootstrap venture. Upon completion of this dynamic training, you'll be awarded your **B.S.diploma** (Bootstrap Strategy)

B. Bootstrapper's Bivouac, Intensive Training
5 days of advanced hands-on training for the front-line entrepreneur. Complete your **M.B.A*** with this dynamic fast paced education in practical life skills.
*Master of Business Audacity

These innovative training events are presented by nationally known motivational consultants. Call us at **319-354-7515** to register for these powerful events. You can reach us by E-Mail at ICANWORK @ .AOL.com

Take action *today*. Hesitation kills dreams.

3. Since most bootstrap ventures are undercapitalized during the start up years, we offer for your new enterprise, **Bootstrapper's Business Services.**

It's very difficult for most bootstrap organizations to hire expensive professional accounting, legal and marketing services. Through our **Bootstrapper's Business Services,** we offer insurance, basic accounting, legal referral, guerrilla marketing tactical guidance, project planning and consulting. You'll save with co-op bulk purchase of these needed services. This is a great way to maximize resources.

4. Bootstrapper's Global Network Central
Setting up your own Internet home page can be expensive. You can have all of the advantages of Global Electronic Commerce by listing the goods or services offered by your bootstrap organization for a fraction of the cost of an individual Internet site.

5. The Bootstrapper's "Bank" is a mutual credit union being set up *by and for* start-up entrepreneurs. We'll work together to create access to working capital.

6. Bootstrapper's Innovation Zone- This is our entrepreneurial idea incubator. This centrally located facility provides lower cost co-op office space, warehousing and plant facilities for start up ventures.

Don't hesitate to contact us for the support that you need. You can call the author direct at #319-354-7515 .

Bootstrapper's Basic Skill #12: Network! Building alliances with other bootstrappers increases your prospects for success greatly. The opposite of net work is not work! Build support networks wherever you go. *Let the whole world know what you are doing.* LIGHT YOUR CANDLE. Put it on a high pedestal in full view.

Reader's notes:

If you want to be a bootstrapper, it's important to take decisive action. Write down below your thoughts as you complete this book. Now, what are <u>you</u> going to do?

Are you now ready to pursue your dream?

List any fears that still stand in your way:

How can I summon the courage to conquer my fears?

What action can I take <u>today</u> to move toward my goals?

There are no excuses for inaction. Get busy today, *whoever* you are, *wherever* you are, with *whatever* you have. The main responsibility of life is *action*. Whether you succeed on a grand scale is not relevant. The fact that you give an *all out attempt* is foremost.

I send my love, respect and encouragement to you.

-MICHAEL RICHARDS, AUTHOR

INNOVATION PRESS is ready to receive manuscripts to review for publication from other bootstrappers, entrepreneurs and innovators. *Send your work to:*

INNOVATION PRESS
P.O.Box 975
Iowa City, Iowa 52244

Bootstrapper's Basic Skill Review

Basic Skill #1: Always place the highest priority on investing in your own self-worth. Nothing else pays a higher return. *You are your most valuable asset.*

Basic Skill #2: Start now! Doubt and procrastination are the major enemies of the bootstrap entrepreneur. *Conquer doubt and inaction with decisive, bold action.*

Basic Skill #3: If a door shuts, climb through the window. If a flood rises, build a raft. If a barrier is built in your path, tunnel under it, go around it, climb over it, or tear it down. *By-pass all barriers.*

Basic Skill #4: Accept deferred gratification. In the early development of making your dream a reality, accept the *joy* of your work as your main pay. Outer rewards of financial freedom, maybe even fame will come your way if you persevere. When these external rewards do come, they will never have as great of value as the original joy and satisfaction derived from the pursuit of your own dream against all odds. The primary reward for work well done is simply more work. *Let work be your love, and joy be your pay!*

Basic Skill #5: Without the passion of enthusiastic commitment, you won't have the energy to transform your dream into reality. *Make a total commitment.*

Basic Skill #6: There are physical materials, creative ideas, time and knowledge being wasted all around you. Re-capture this waste, recycle it into innovative, productive use. *Discover the resources all around you.*

Basic Skill #7: Base all of your work on love: Love of yourself, love of your work, love of your co-workers and love of customers you serve. Love connects us all with a deep ocean of energy. Live, laugh, work and love in abundance. *Love is the source of real wealth.*

Basic Skill #8: Teamwork is the basis of all success. Success never happens alone. The people involved in your organization are your most important asset. Invest in the self-worth of yourself and your entire team. When a bootstrapper gives everything they've got to their working team, your team will give everything they've got also. No matter what your business, *building your team is your primary business.*

Basic Skill #9: Make adversity your ally. Within every problem lie unclaimed jewels of opportunity. Become a master at finding this value. Find the absurdity in all adversity. *Keep laughing 'til you win.*

Basic Skill #10: Build your work on a strong spiritual foundation. Fearless faith will get you through all obstacles placed in your path. *Faith works.*

Basic Skill #11: Entrepreneurs who keep a lively interest in health, family, community, sports and the arts thrive. A person who lives a healthy, balanced life will have the energy to create and produce in five hours what a burned out workaholic can in fifteen hours. *Live a balanced life.* Life is your main business.

Basic Skill #12: Network! Building alliances with other bootstrappers increases your prospects for success greatly. The opposite of net work is *not work*. Build support networks wherever you go. *Let the whole world know what you are doing.* Light your candle!

These **12 basic skills** can be utilized by bootstrappers in any field of human endeavor. Michael Richards, author of *Light One Candle*, has established a unique consulting service, **I.C.A.N.** (International Creative Ability Network) I.C.A.N. was created to provide special training for social entrepreneurs, agencies, and communities that wish to start ventures that create community wealth for disabled and disadvantaged persons. Candleworks was created as a *model* in action.

I-can

2920 Industrial Park Road
Iowa City, Iowa 52240, U.S.A.

A creative resource to activate ability within disability and to develop the advantage beyond disadvantage.

MARKETING

PLANNING

TEAM-BUILDING

SKILL DEVELOPMENT

We organize the building blocks for business success; so you can say with confidence: "I-can".

Seventy percent of all disadvantaged and disabled persons in the U.S. are unemployed. The goal of **I-can** is to change this situation through the creation of viable self-employment options. **I-can** is action oriented. **I-can** works.

I-can provides a comprehensive professional training resource for disadvantaged and disabled persons who choose to develop a creative business venture.

I-can is a dynamic team of business professionals. We provide consulting, training, follow-up and evaluation. We provide services to disabled and disadvantaged persons who are ready to take an entrepreneurial approach to develop economic self-sufficiency.

I-can service menu:

1. Business Feasibility Studies
2. Goal Development/Focus
3. Business Plan Preparation
4. Project Start-up Consultation
5. Business Growth Strategy
6. Effective Marketing Methods
7. Legal and Accounting Referral
8. Computer/Internet System Design
9. Human Resource Development
10. Business Performance Evaluation

The **I-can** consulting team includes business operations professionals, human resource trainers, marketing advisors, computer systems consultants and referrals to accounting and legal help.

Our fees are billed on an hourly basis. **I-can** fees will reflect the specific service mix required by each project.

I-Can Professional Profiles:

MIKE RICHARDS, I-CAN LEAD CONSULTANT
For 25 years he has provided training and consulting for businesses that range from start ups to the Fortune 500. Michael Richards is presently the C.E.O. and Operations Director of Candleworks, an entrepreneurial industry that has gained international recognition for creating a dynamic business organization operated by a motivated group of disabled and disadvantaged persons. Candleworks was recognized as "Best Practice" in Community Economic Development by President Clinton at the National Conference of Mayors. Mike has written business plans for various projects through the SBDC at the University of Iowa and the "Fast Track" program at the Center for Entrepreneurship. Mike is on the Advisory Board of the Institute for Social and Economic Development. ISED offers consultation and training for micro-enterprise start-ups.

Mike is the author of "Light One Candle", *A Handbook for bootstrapping entrepreneurs* (INNOVATION PRESS) He is also a frequent speaker on entrepreneurship for colleges and community groups around the U.S. Mike has provided consulting and training for groups all over the United States, Canada and Europe.

LYNETTE RICHARDS AND JANE BURDEN ARE I-CAN'S HUMAN RESOURCE TRAINERS

Lynette has served as human resource director for large retail and service organizations in New York. Lynette is the co-founder of Candleworks. Jane is an experiential training specialist and team building expert. Jane has designed and delivered experiential training for major business organizations and as a staff member of Princeton University's Blairstown Center.

WENDY GERMAIN, MARKETING STRATEGY

For 20 years, Wendy has developed marketing strategy for major business and non-profit organizations. Wendy was a founding member of Lotus Development Corporation, and a driving force in the marketing of Lotus 123 software to the global market. Wendy developed a national catalog of products created by disadvantaged and disabled persons for The Better Homes Fund. Her extensive experience includes market research, trade shows advertising and public relations.

I-Can Professional Referrals:

Professional Consultation: **I-can** refers our clients to appropriate attorneys and accountants in their community to prepare required business documents.

International Creative Ability Network

Phone: 319-354-7515/ Fax 319-337-9034
e-mail: ICANWORK @aol.com

GOING GLOBAL

Every business is now competing in the global marketplace. The internet has provides a link to goods and services from any point in the world.

You can accept your position in the global economy passively, by default, or you can build a global perspective into your plan of action.

By participating in our Bootstrapper's Global Network Central, you can be link in to the internet as part of an entrepreneur's co-op home page. This will present your products, ideas, or services to the global market for a very reasonable cost. Contact us to participate.

Candleworks has developed alliances with creative entrepreneurs in Europe, The Caribbean, Latin America via our home page at WWW.Candleworks.Org

Light One Candle.
Let your line shine all over the earth.

ORDER FORM FOR ADDITIONAL COPIES OF THIS BOOK

Share *"Light One Candle"* with students, family, friends and business associates!

PHOTO COPY THIS FORM AND SEND IN by FAX or MAIL

Fax orders: 319-337-9034   Phone orders: Call 319-354-7515

Internet Orders (books *and* candles): **WWW.CandlworksOrg**

Postal Orders: Innovation Press, P.O.Box 975, Ia.City,IA 52244

Please Ship: _____ x $9.95 U.S. =_$_____
                #copies   x $14.50 CAN   Total Purchase

Tax: Please add 6.25% for Iowa sales tax $_____

                      Add Shipping Cost$_____
         ($4 for 1st book, $2 for each additional book)

                      Grand Total $_____

Credit Card # _____

         Visa_____   Master Card_____

Name on Card_____ Exp. Date_____/____

Ship to: Name:_____

Company Name:_____

Address: _____

City:_____ State:_____Postal Code_____

Telephone: _____E-Mail:_____

IF YOU ARE INTERESTED IN SUPPORTING THE IMPORTANT WORK OF CANDLEWORKS, THE MOST DIRECT WAY IS TO **ORDER** OUR QUALITY CANDLES!

To order candles, **photocopy** and **enlarge** the form on the next page.

150

RETAIL ORDER FORM
Master Card or Visa #
_____
Exp. Date_____
Name on credit card_____

CANDLEWORKS
P.O. Box 975
Iowa City, IA 52244
To Order:
Ph.:319-337-6316
Fax:319-337-9034

CandleWorks Aromatherapy Candles	BURN TIME hrs	Romance	Vitality	Serenity	Body Balance	Breathe Free	Tension Tamer	Moon Tide	# ORDERED	Price Per Unit	Total Dollars
Frosted Glass	25									8.30	
2 oz. Refill	12									2.00	
3x4 Pillar	48									8.30	
2 oz. Refills Variety 4 Pack	48	Assortment of 4 Scents (Romance, Vitality, Serenity, and Tension Tamer)								9.50	
2 oz. Refills Variety 4 Pack	48	Assortment of 4 Scents (Body Balance, Breathe Free, Tension Tamer, and Moontide)								9.50	
12" Tapers, -2	10									5.00	
14 oz. Apothecary	72									12.50	
4 oz. Travel Tin	20									5.90	

CandleWorks Private Label Home Fragrance Ensemble,
"Scents of the Seasons"

3.5 oz. Glass	20	"Spring-time Rain" Fragrance in Green Glass				7.30
3.5 oz. Glass	20	"Summer Sojourn" Fragrance in Yellow Glass				7.30
3.5 oz. Glass	20	"Heartland Harvest" Fragrance in Ruby Red Glass				7.30
3.5 oz. Glass	20	"Winter Memories" Fragrance in Cobalt Blue Glass				7.30
Gift Ensemble	80	Deluxe Package of All Four "Scents of the Seasons" Listed Above				29.50

"Odor Eraser" CandleWorks Room Freshening Candles

"Smoke-Away"		Light Blue	Natural	Light Rose	Light Green	
Votives	12					2.00
3x4 Pillar	48					7.70
Apothecary Jar	72	All Apothecary Smoke-Away Candles are Poured with Natural Color Wax				12.50
"Pet So-Fresh"		Light Blue	Natural	Light Rose	Light Green	
Votives	12					2.00
3x4	48					7.70
Apothecary Jar	72	All Apothecary Pet So-Fresh are Poured with Natural Color Wax				12.50
"Kitchen Clear"		Light Blue	Natural	Light Rose	Light Green	
Votives	12					2.00
3x4	48					7.70
Apothecary Jar	72	All Apothecary Kitchen Clear Candles are Poured with Natural Color Wax				12.50

"Bath & Boudoir", Candlelight Bath Ensemble: a Two-piece Stacked Set of Frosted Glass Containers, with a 48-hour Fragranced Candle in the Large Container and Matching Scented Bath Salts in the Small Container

"A Quiet Moment" in Frosted Ivory Glass, A Relaxing Blend Ylang-Ylang, Vetiver, and Lavender	22.90
"Romantic Interlude" in Frosted Rose Glass, A Blend of Patchouli, Frankincense, and Sandalwood	22.90
"Refreshing" in Frosted Sea-Blue Glass, A Lively Blend of Bergamot, and Juniper Berry Fragrance	22.90

Ship To :	phone #:	
Address:	City, State, Zip code	Product Total:
mail in checks or cash $15 minimum purchase	Please add 10% for shipping- $3.50 minimum shipping fee	Shipping Cost: Grand Total:

THIS BOOK IS THE STORY OF CANDLEWORKS
Business Profile

1. We've created 30 permanent jobs for people that had been left out of the employment market in our community: former welfare moms, homeless families, at risk youth, work release workers from the corrections dept., mentally and physically disabled persons. Candleworks engages each person's *ability to overcome their disability*. Candleworks was named Business of the Year by the Iowa City Human Rights Commission for our innovative work with people in need. Candleworks has been featured in many regional and national print and television news reports including CBS THIS MORNING. Candleworks provides interest free loans for rent and deposits. We have assisted 20 families with rental housing, and have provided assistance for two families to become home owners in a cooperative effort with City Housing.

2. This diverse group work together to create quality candle products for some of America's most progressive merchants: Hy Vee Groceries, Aura Cacia, The Body Shop, Wild Oats Natural Markets, Ben and Jerry's, Urban Outfitters, and Candleman Stores. Candleworks has created custom candles for Redbook Magazine, New York fashion designer, Eileen Fisher and special mantle candles for the Holiday T.V. Special, "Martha Stewart Living". Everyone who works at Candleworks is part of a quality team. We have a very innovative employee structure. All of our middle management positions have been recruited *from the bottom up*; our quality work team supervisors include disabled or formerly homeless persons who were brought back into the employment market and trained at Candleworks.

3. Candleworks creates economic development through innovation for our community. Since we sell our products in all 50 states, all provinces in Canada and Europe, the one million dollars in revenue generated this year by Candleworks will be new money

introduced into the local economy from outside sources. Because of this community economic benefit, Candleworks was the first business that our city government ever sponsored for an economic development grant. In just the first 6 months of our grant, we paid a quarter of a million dollars in payroll to low income people in our community. That's a rapid return on the $50,000 CBDG investment in Candleworks.

4. Candleworks was one of the first companies in the world to make innovative candles from vegetable waxes for the natural products market *(most candles are made from petroleum and animal by-products)*. Candleworks has been sought out by natural product giants like Wild Oats Markets, Aura Cacia, Body Shop Biolage/Matrix (a division of Bristol Meyer Squib).

5. Candleworks has been built up from nothing to an important employer by building a manufacturing plant through an innovative bootstrap approach. Much of our processing equipment we have designed and assembled ourselves from recycled components from plants that had been shut down. We recycle all of our packing materials. Candleworks *recycles materials and rebuilds lives.* We've made a lot happen with very little resources. Candleworks started in a tiny abandoned building with no running water or electricity. We now operate in a modern 10,000 square foot plant in our city's industrial park.

6. Candleworks competes with the largest candle manufacturers in the world through "guerrilla marketing" and global internet retailing. The Federal HUD Office and President Clinton awarded Candleworks the "Best Practice Award" at the National Conference of Mayors. Our company is working to redefine civic responsibility and business ethics for the new millennium. Candleworks provides a model for other communities to follow. We offer innovative consulting to groups to develop economic development initiatives.

Candleworks welcomes tour groups. Come and visit!